WORLD'S GREAT AUTHORS AND POETS

Published by
Lotus Press Publishers & Distributors

World's Great Authors and Poets

Jasvinder Kaur

4735/22, Prakash Deep Building
Ansari Road, Darya Ganj,
New Delhi - 110002

Lotus Press : Publishers & Distributors
Unit No. 220, 2nd Floor, 4735/22, Prakash Deep Building,
Ansari Road, Darya Ganj, New Delhi- 110002
Ph.: 23280047, 98118-38000
• E-mail : lotuspress1984@gmail.com
www.lotuspress.co.in

World's Great Authors and Poets

ISBN: 978-81-8382-251-0

Printed & Published by : **Lotus Press Publishers & Distributors,** New Delhi-02

PREFACE

All around the world millions of authors and poets describe about the whole generation. An author is a person who originates or gives existence to anything and that authorship determines responsibility for what is created.

India has produced several great writers who inspired the coming generations by their writings. Their work vividly portrays the picture of Indian society and subtly brings out the ills of it. Indian writers have played a progress part in the reformation of society.

Indian writers have distinguished themselves not only in traditional Indian languages but also in English. Indian writers have established a place in the fiction category as well. Many of their Books have gone on to become Bestsellers not only in India but around the world. V S Naipaul, Salman Rushdie, Arundhati Roy and Kiran Desai have won the prestigious Man Booker Prize, with Salman Rushdie going on to win the Booker of Bookers. If you haven't yet had a bite of Indian literature or would like to read some more, in this book there is a list of some of the Best Indian Fiction you must read.

In this book, biographies of several world poets and authors are being highlighted.

One question that people usuallies ask is " why one

writes or reads a biography". And the answer is to read about the history of an individual's personal life about the great writers and legends' life. The book aims to endeavor the maximum knowledge about the great writers who writes for us and played important role in our history.

-Author

CONTENTS

- *Preface* ... *v*

1. Ved Vyas ... 11
2. Kalidasa ... 13
3. Tulsidas ... 17
4. Valmiki ... 20
5. Rumi ... 22
6. William Shakespeare ... 25
7. Jonathan Swift ... 28
8. Sir Walter Scott ... 31
9. Nagarjuna ... 34
10. William Wordsworth ... 37
11. William Makepeace Thackeray ... 40
12. Harriet Beecher Stowe ... 43
13. John Ruskin ... 47
14. Walt Whitman ... 50
15. George Eliot ... 54
16. Leo Tolstoy ... 57
17. Lewis Carroll ... 61
18. Mark Twain ... 64

19. Bankim Chandra Chatterjee ... 67
20. Thomas Hardy ... 71
21. Ella Wheeler Wilcox ... 74
22. Arthur Conan Doyle ... 77
23. Rabindranath Tagore ... 80
24. Rudyard Kipling ... 83
25. Sri Aurobindo ... 87
26. Somerset Maugham ... 91
27. Sarojini Naidu ... 94
28. Premchand ... 97
29. Virginia Woolf ... 100
30. Khalil Gibran ... 104
31. Sinclair Lewis ... 107
32. Sukumar Roy ... 110
33. Jaishankar Prasad ... 113
34. Pearl S. Buck ... 116
35. Suryakant Tripathi 'Nirala' ... 118
36. Nirad C. Chaudhuri ... 120
37. Thornton Wilder ... 124
38. Subhadra Kumari Chauhan ... 127
39. Mulk Raj Anand ... 129
40. Jim Thompson ... 132
41. R. K. Narayan ... 135

42. Mahadevi Varma ... 137
43. Harivansh Rai Bachchan ... 139
44. Robert A Heinlein ... 142
45. Ramdhari Singh Dinkar ... 145
46. Saadat Hasan Manto ... 147
47. Michael Gilbert ... 148
48. Dylan Thomas ... 151
49. Laurie Lee ... 156
50. Khushwant Singh ... 159
51. Judith Wright ... 161
52. Kaifi Azmi ... 165
53. R. K. Laxman ... 167
54. James Jones ... 169
55. Kingsley Amis ... 172
56. Alistair Maclean ... 175
57. Norman Mailer ... 179
58. Mahasweta Devi ... 182
59. James Wright ... 185
60. Elie Wiesel ... 188
61. A. K. Ramanujan ... 190
62. Sri Chinmoy ... 193
63. V.s. Naipaul ... 195
64. Manoj Das ... 197

65. Shashi Deshpande ... 199

66. Bapsi Sidhwa ... 200

67. Girish Karnad ... 202

68. Bharati Mukherjee ... 205

69. Anne Tyler ... 207

70. Vikas Swarup ... 210

71. Shobha De ... 212

72. Salman Rushdie ... 214

73. Vikram Seth ... 217

74. Amitav Ghosh ... 220

75. Gita Sahgal ... 223

76. Namita Gokhale ... 225

77. Manil Suri ... 227

78. Vikram Chandra ... 229

79. Anita Rau Badami ... 231

80. Arundhati Roy ... 233

81. Amit Chaudhuri ... 236

82. Vijay Singh ... 238

83. Jhumpa Lahiri ... 241

84. Pankaj Mishra ... 244

85. Kiran Desai ... 246

VED VYAS

Author of the great epic Mahabharata, Ved Vyas was the first and greatest acharya of Hindu Dharma. He is responsible for classifying the four Vedas, wrote the 18 puranas and recited the Mahabharata. In fact, the Mahabharata is often called as the fifth Veda. Its most important and the most glorified section is the Bhagwad Gita, the lesson given to Arjuna by Lord Krishna on the battlefield. The biography of Ved Vyas is very vivid and makes an interesting read.

Around some 5000 years ago, he was born on an island on the holy river Yamuna. His father was Rishi Parashar, a sage, and his mother was Satyavati. He taught the Vedas to his pupils with ardent devotion and dedication. It is said that Mahabharata is the 18th puran a that was written by Ved Vyas. He fathered four famous sons: Pandu, Dhritarashtra, Vidur and Sukhdev. Ved Vyas received knowledge from great sages like Vasudeva and Sanakadikas. He described that the most important goal in one's life was to attain Narayana or the Divine Supreme.

Apart from the Mahabharata, he also wrote the Brahmasutra, one of his shortest theologies on Hindu philosophy. It is said that Ved Vyas is immortal and he never died. Seeing the widespread violence in today's times, he is said to have retreated into some remote village in Northern India. The life of Ved Vyas is an example to all in the modern times on how to be selfless and devote oneself entirely to the Lord in order to attain Nirvana.

Vyas does not signify the name of any one person. It is a title. Ved Vyas, the author of the Mahabharata, is called 'Ved Vyas' because it was he who classified the Vedas into four branches. His hermitage was in Badari and he was therefore known as 'Badarayana'. According to mythology, Vyasa grew into manhood shortly after his birth and was well versed in the Shastras, the Puranas, poetry, history and other branches of learning. He was ripe in wisdom. Then he left for Badari for his tapasya. Later, he took his mother Satyavati in the forest to spend the last days of her life there.

Without Vyas, there would have been no Kauravas, no Pandavas and no Mahabharata War–or the Mahabharata story, either. It was Vyas himself who gave the story of Mahabharata to mankind. It is said that it was Lord Brahma who motivated him to write the story of the Mahabharata with the help of Lord Ganesha. He saw the rise of quite a number of powerful kings and dynasties. Being a 'rishi' who could live for hundreds of years, it is believed that he is still living in Badari.

KALIDASA

One of the greatest Sanskrit poets that India has ever had, the life history of Kalidasa is absolutely fascinating and interesting. Though the exact time of his fame is not known, it is estimated that he lived around the middle of the 4th or 5th century A.D. This is roughly the period of the reign of the famous Chandragupta, the successor of Kumaragupta. An insight into the biography of the great Indian poet Kalidasa provides us with an immense amount of detailed information about the places he travelled and the kind of life he led.

The poems he wrote were usually of epic proportions and were written in classical Sanskrit. His creations were used for fine arts like music and dance. Regarded as an outstanding writer, Kalidasa resided at the palace of Chandragupta in Pataliputra (modern day Patna). He was one of the gems of the court of Chandragupta. According to legends, Kalidasa was blessed with good looks. This attracted a princess with whom he fell in love. Since Kalidasa was not too good in intellect and wit, the princess rejected him. He then worshipped the Goddess Kali and she blessed him with intellect and wit, thus making him one of the "nine gems" in the court of Chandragupta.

Perhaps the most famous and beautiful work of Kalidasa is the *Shakuntalam*. It is the second play of Kalidasa after he wrote *Malavikagnimitra*. The *Shakuntalam* tells the story of king Dushyant who falls in love with a beautiful girl Shakuntala, who happens to be the daughter of a saint.

They get married and lead a happy life until one day, the king was asked to travel somewhere. In his absence, a sage curse Shakuntala as she offended him unknowingly by not acknowledging his presence.

Due to the curse, Dushyant's entire memory is wiped out and he doesn't remember his marriage with Shakuntala. But the sage feels pity for her and gives a solution that he will remember everything if he sees the ring given to her by Dushyant. But she loses the ring one day in the river while bathing. After a series of incidents, a fisherman who finds the ring inside a fish rushes to the king with the ring. The king then recalls everything and rushes to Shakuntala to apologise for his actions. She forgives him and they live happily ever after.

Kalidasa also wrote two epic poems called *Kumarasambhava,* which means birth of Kumara, and the *Raghuvamsha,* which means the dynasty of Raghu. There are also two lyric poems written by Kalidasa known as *Meghadutta* that stands for cloud messenger, and the *Ritusamhara* that means description of the seasons. *Meghaduta* is one of the finest works of Kalidasa in terms of world literature. The beauty of the continuity in flawless Sanskrit is unmatched till date.

One of Kalidasa's greatest works is *'Kumarasambhava'*. Critics maintain that Kalidasa wrote only the first eight chapters of the epic poem. The work describes the marriage of Lord Shiva and his consort Parvati. It begins with a fine description of that giant among mountains, the Himalaya. Kalidasa writes: "Himalaya is rich in life. Living there are the Siddhas. Kinnaras and Vidyadhara beauties. Clouds in front of the caves look like curtains. You can trace the track of lions by looking at the precious stones spilled from the heads of elephants and not by bloodstains. You have to know the paths they tread by recognizing 'Sarala' trees against whose stem the elephants rub themselves attracted by the sweet milk exuded by the trees. All the things needed for a sacrifice ('Yajna') are available here. Brahma (the God of creation) himself has made this the king of the mountains." It is not only a place for lovers who want to find happiness in life; it is also an ideal retreat for those who want to meditate.

Kalidasa's works are known for their triple qualities -- a sense of beauty, a capacity for appreciation of the aesthetic values and our traditional culture. Kalidasa's portrayals of the great Himalayan mountain and of the mode in which the season of spring (vasanta) blossomed, are some of the most lyrical expressions in the language. His descriptions are vivid and heart-warming; it is as if we are seeing the events happening before us. Kalidasa's portrayal of Parvati's grace and beauty magnificently shows his ability as a poet. Rati's lament upon Kama being consigned to flames moves us to tears. Kalidasa is equally at ease in portraying the happy marital life of Shiva and Parvati as a couple deeply in love as also of picturing the grace and beauty of both nature and man, feelings of joy and sorrow and all other emotions.

Crowning all these pen-pictures of things that are beautiful and sweet in life is Kalidasa's extolling of a noble culture. What does 'culture' mean? It is a sense of decent behaviour — in body and mind; it is the blossoming of the mind and heart to savour the rich and colourful beauty around us — such as the colour and fragrance of flowers which gladden the hearts of one and all. The thought, word and action of a man's mature mind give happiness to others. Besides describing these in a masterly style and imagination, Kalidasa also exhibits his powers of perception while recognizing what we can call as 'beauty in action and behaviour.

Kalidasa's poem gives us a vivid picture of what a good, meaningful life is.

TULSIDAS

'Tulsi Ramayana' is a very famous and great epic of North India. It relates the story of Sri Rama. It was written by Goswami Tulsidas. (Goswami means one who has renounced the world and has become a sanyasi, that is, an ascetic.) That is why it was popularly known as Tulsi Ramayana.

Tulsidas gave it the title, 'Ramacharitamanasa'.

Valmiki, the first poet, told the story of Sri Rama in his 'Ramayana'; after him hundreds of poets have retold it in their own way. 'Tulsi Ramayana' is one of the most popular and venerated Ramayanas.

Many poets of our country were saints. They were great scholars as well as great devotees. They lived as rishis. Goswami Tulsidas too was a great scholar well versed in Vedic lore, philosophy and mythology. People say that Tulsidas, by virtue of his perfect devotion, was so fortunate as to meet Anjaneya, the renowned servant of Sri Rama. It is said Anjaneya helped him to see with his own eyes Sri Rama and Lakshmana. Tulsidas declared: 'Bhakti is the only way leading to God's grace. Sri Rama is the Supreme God (Parabrahma). He is the ideal man. And he is the Lord of this world. His words and deeds themselves form the code of human conduct in this world.'

In his 'Ramayana' Tulsidas has narrated the story of Sri Rama; he has also taught the principles of right living through different characters. The lessons taught in that work are valid to this day.

The epic gives beautiful pictures of the right relation between father and children, and of the affection among brothers. It also shows how the husband and the wife, mothera-in-law and daughtera-in-law, should conduct themselves. Tulsidas describes the affection of a teacher for his disciples and the respect of the disciples for their teacher. But his poem is not just a moral piece. Tulsidas has narrated the story of Sri Rama in a moving and delightful way. As we read it we feel as if we see Rama, Seeta and Lakshmana before our very eyes.

The Age of Tulsidas

Goswami Tulsidas was born at the close of the 15th century and lived upto the beginning of the 17th century. It was a bad period for the Hindus. They had lost their freedom and had to struggle hard to maintain their unity. All their scriptures were in Sanskrit, so many people found them difficult to understand.

As the Hindus had no freedom, it was difficult for them even to attempt to expound the ideas of their religion. Women and also some groups among the Hindus did not have equality. This state of affairs made gifted and liberal-minded poets unhappy.

Sri Ramananda was a disciple of Sri Ramanujacharya, the founder of the Srivaishnava faith. He and his disciples lived in North India. He opened the doors of 'Bhakti' (devotion) to all and brought hope into the lives of the masses.

It was at this time that Sri Ramananda spread the cult of Rama Bhakti by preaching that Rama is the protector of all people. Saint Kabirdas extolled the greatness of 'Rama – the formless God' saying that Ram and Rahim were not different. Thus he tried to bring about unity among the Hindus and the Muslims.

Sri Tulsidas set before the people the image of Sri Rama as all virtuous, all powerful, the Lord of the World, and the very embodiment of the Supreme Reality (Parabrahma). He gave them the light of 'Bhakti' and thus dispelled the darkness of fear from their minds. Sri Rama shone as an ideal man and the protector.

Tulsidas formed a brotherhood of the devotees of Rama. He sang and composed songs. He wrote books and preached to people. Though he was learned in Sanskrit, he composed poetry in the languages the people spoke. They were only different dialects of Hindi used in North India. He wrote for the common man and not for the learned, it was in the languages actually used by the people that he gave talks and discourses glorifying Bhakti.

Tulsidas was a great man. He suffered much hardship from his early years. He did not know the care and affection of father and mother. He was brought up by the charity of the people. Even after he became a sanyasi, difficulties did not cease. When he settled down in Kashi, many blamed him, and many made fun of him. But he was always patient and calm. Once he said, "Some say that Tulsi does bad deeds. Some call him a big cheat. Some others say that he truly is a devotee of Rama. I can bear all comments. My mind is untroubled. Whatever is to happen to Tulsi, good or bad, is in the hands of Rama."

Tulsidas was a very great scholar. He had made a profound study of Indian philosophy and literature. But his scholarship did not make him arrogant. For him meditation on Rama was more important than all other things. Whatever the difficulties one should not lose zest in life. One should always do good to others, treating all as the children of God, making no distinction of caste, status or rank. This was the way he showed to others and this was how he himself lived.

VALMIKI

Maharishi Valmiki claims the distinction of being the author of the holy epic 'Ramayana', consisting of 24,000 verses. He is also believed to be the author of *Yoga Vasistha,* a text that elaborates on a range of philosophical issues. Written approximately 5000 years ago, it was taught to Lord Rama when he lost all the hopes in life.

Maharishi Valmiki was born as Ratnakara to sage Prachetasa. At a very young age, Ratnakara went into the forest and got lost. A hunter, who was passing by, saw Ratnakara and took him under his own care. Under the love and care of his foster parents, Ratnakara forgot his original parents. Under his father's guidance, Ratnakara turned out to be an excellent hunter. As he approached marriageable age, Ratnakara was married to a beautiful girl from the hunter's family.

As his family grew larger, Ratnakara found it next to impossible to feed them. As a result, he took to robbery and began looting people passing from one village to another. One day, the great sage Narada, while passing through the jungle, was attacked by Ratnakara. As Narada played his Veena and sang praises of the Lord, he saw a transformation coming over Ratnakara. Then, he asked Ratnakara whether the family, for whom he was robbing others, will partake in his sins also. Ratnakara went to ask the question to his family and on being refused by all his family members, he went back to sage Narada. Narada taught him the sacred name of 'Rama' and asked him to sit in meditation, chanting the name of Rama, till the time Narada came back.

Ratnakara followed the instructions and kept sitting in a meditative posture for years, during which his body got completely covered by an anthill. At last, Narada came to see him and removed all the anthills from his body. Then, he told Ratnakara that his *tapasya* (meditation) paid off and the God was pleased with him. Ratnakara was bestowed with the honour of a Brahmarshi and given the name of Valmiki, since he was reborn from the Valmika (the ant-hill). Sage Valmiki founded his ashram at the banks of River Ganga.

One day, Valmiki had the fortuity of receiving Lord Rama, his wife Sita and brother Lakshman at his ashram. On Valmiki's suggestion, Lord Rama built his hut on Chitrakuta hill, near the ashram.

Narada visited Maharishi Valmiki in his ashram once and there, he narrated the story of Lord Rama. Thereafter he received a vision from Brahma in which the Lord instructed him to write the Ramayana in shlokas, which the sage readily followed.

It is said that Valmiki taught the Ramayana to the sons of Rama, Luv and Kush. He is also said to have given shelter to Sita after she was banished from the kingdom. The Ramayana is sung rather than just recited. Those who have read the Ramayana have bowed to Valmiki with great respect. It is said that when Luv and Kush were singing the Ramayana in their sweet voices in front of Rama, he himself was unaware of the fact that they were his own sons!

RUMI

(1207 – 17.12.1273)

Maulana Jalaluddin Rumi was a 13th century Persian poet, an Islamic dervish and a Sufi mystic. He is regarded as one of the greatest spiritual masters and poetical intellects. Born in 1207 AD, he belonged to a family of learned theologians. He made use of everyday life's circumstances to describe the spiritual world. Rumi's poems have acquired immense popularity, especially among the Persian speakers of Afghanistan, Iran and Tajikistan. Numerous poems written by the great poet have been translated into different languages.

Jalaluddin Rumi was born on September 30, 1207, in Balkh (in present-day Afghanistan). His father, Bahaduddin Walad, was a theologian, jurist and a mystic, while his mother was Mumina Khatun. When Mongols invaded Central Asia, between 1215 and 1220, Rumi left Balkh with his family and a group of disciples. The migrating caravan travelled extensively in Muslim lands, including Baghdad, Damascus, Malatya, Erzincan, Sivas, Kayseri and Nigde. After performing pilgrimage in Mecca, they eventually settled in Konya, located in present-day western Turkey. At that time, Rumi's father was an Islamic theologian, a teacher and a preacher.

Rumi was a disciple of Sayyed Burhan ud-Din Muhaqqiq Termazi, one of his father's students. Under the guidance of Sayyed Termazi, he practiced Sufism and acquired a lot of knowledge about spiritual matters and secrets of the spirit world. After the demise of Bahaduddin in 1231 AD, Rumi inherited his father's position and became a prominent religious teacher. He preached in the mosques of Konya. By the time Rumi reached the age of 24, he had proven himself as a well-informed scholar in the field of religious science.

Rumi was already a teacher and a theologian, when in 1244 AD he came across a wandering dervish named Shamsuddin of Tabriz. The meeting proved to be a turning point in his life. Shamsuddin and Rumi became very close friends. Shams went to Damascus, where he was allegedly killed by the students of Rumi who were resentful of their close relationship. Rumi expressed his love for Shamsuddin and grief at his death, through music, dance and poems.

For nearly ten years after meeting Shamsuddin, Rumi devoted himself to writing ghazals. He made a compilation of ghazals and named it *Diwan-e-Kabir* or *Diwan-e Shams-e Tabrizi.* Thereafter, Rumi encountered a goldsmith – Salaud-Din-e Zarkub – whom he made his companion. When Salaud-Din-e Zarkub died, Rumi befriended one of his favourite disciples named Hussam-e Chalabi. Rumi spent most of the later years of his life in Anatolia, where he finished six volumes of his masterwork, the *Masnavi.*

Diwan-e Shams-e Tabrizi (or *Diwan-e-Kabir*) is one of the masterpieces of Rumi. It is a collection of ghazals named in the honour of dervish Shamsuddin, who was Rumi's great friend and inspiration. It also contains an assortment of poems arranged according to the rhyming scheme. *Diwan-e Kabir* has been written in 'Dari' dialect. It is regarded as one of the greatest works of Persian literature.

Mathnawi is a compilation of six volumes of poetry, written in a didactic style. The poems are intended to inform, instruct as well as entertain the reader. It is believed that Rumi started the work of *Mathnawi* at the suggestion of his then companion, Hussam al-Din Chalabi. *Mathnawi* attempts to explain the various facets of spiritual life.

Rumi's popularity has gone beyond national and ethnic borders. He is considered to be one of the classical poets, by the speakers of Persian language in Iran, Afghanistan and Tajikistan. For many years, he had a great influence on Turkish literature. The popularity of his works inspired many artists, including Mohammad Reza Shajarian (Iran), Shahram Nazeri (Iran), Davood Azad (Iran) and Ustad Mohammad Hashem Cheshti (Afghanistan), to give classical interpretation for his poems. Rumi's works have been translated into many languages across the world, including Russian, German, Urdu, Turkish, Arabic, French, Italian and Spanish.

Rumi departed from the world on 17th December 1273 AD, in Konya, within the Seljuk Empire's territory (currently within Turkey). He was buried beside his father in Konya. A tomb named Mevlana mausoleum was built in Konya, commemorating the great Sufi poet. It consists of a mosque, dervish living quarters and a dance hall. The sacred site is visited by his admirers coming from different parts of the world.

WILLIAM SHAKESPEARE

(26.04.1564 – 23.04.1616)

English poet, dramatist, and actor, William Shakespeare is considered by many to be the greatest dramatist of all time. Some of Shakespeare's plays, such as *Hamlet* and *Romeo and Juliet,* are among the most famous literary works of the world. However, his early works did not match the artistic quality of Marlowe's dramas. Ben Jonson (1572-1637), another contemporary playwright, wrote that Shakespeare's "wit was in his own power; would the rule of it had been so too."

There is not much record of Shakespeare´s personal life. Rumours arise from time to time that he did not write his plays, and the real author was Christopher Marlowe, Queen Elizabeth or Edward De Vere (1550-1604), whom T.J. Looney identified in 1920 as the author of Shakespeare's plays. A large body of 'Oxfordians' have since built on this claim and the reluctance to believe that a man of humble origins could be such a great author. According to some numerologists, Shakespeare wrote the King James Version of the Bible at the age of 46. Their "evidence": Shake is the 46th word of the 46th Psalm, Spear is the 46th word from the end in the 46th Psalm.

William Shakespeare was born in Stratford-upon-Avon, a small countrytown. Stratford was famous for its malting. The black plague killed in 1564 one out of seven of the town's 1,500 inhabitants. Shakespeare was the eldest son of Mary Arden, the daughter of a local landowner, and her husband, John Shakespeare (c. 1530-1601), a glover and wood dealer. John Aubrey (1626-1697) tells in *Brief Lives* that

Shakespeare's father was a butcher and the young William exercised his father's trade, "but when he kill'd a Calfe he would do it in a high style, and make a speech." In 1568 John Shakespeare was made the Mayor of Stratford and a justice of peace. His wool business failed in the 1570s, and in 1580 he was fined £40, with other 140 men, for failing to find surety to keep the peace. There is no record that his fine was paid. Later the church commissioners reported of him and eight other men that they had failed to attend church "for fear of process for debt". The family's position was restored in the 1590s by earnings of William Shakespeare, and in 1596 he was awarded a coat of arms.

Very little is known about Shakespeare's early life, and his later works have inspired a number of interpretations. T.S. Eliot wrote that "I would suggest that none of the plays of Shakespeare has a "meaning," although it would be equally false to say that a play of Shakespeare is "meaningless." Shakespeare is assumed to have been educated at Stratford Grammar School, and he may have spent the years 1580-82 as a teacher for the Roman Catholic Houghton family in Lancashire.

When Shakespeare was 15, a woman from a nearby village got drowned in the Avon. Her death was ruled accidental but it may have been a suicide. Later in *Hamlet* Shakespeare left open the question whether Ophelia died accidentally or by her own hand. At the age of 18, Shakespeare married a local girl, Anne Hathaway (died 1623), who was eight years older. Their first child, Susannah, was born within six months, and twins Hamnet and Judith were born in 1585. Hamnet, Shakespeare's only son, died in 1596, at the age of 11. It has often been suggested, that the lines in King John, beginning with "Grief fills the room of my absent child", reflects Shakespeare's grief.

Shakespeare was known in his day as a very rapid writer: "His mind and hand went together," his publishers Heminges and Condell reported, "and what he thought, he uttered with that easiness that we have scarce received from him a blot in his papers." Despite all the praise, some writer's were not enthusiastic about his plays. Samuel Pepys (1633-1703) called *A Midsummer Night's Dream* "the most insipid, ridiculous play that I ever saw in my life." Voltaire wrote: "Shakespeare is a drunken savage with some imagination whose plays please only in London and Canada," "Shakespeare is the Corneille of London, but everywhere else he is a great fool..."

Shakespeare wrote also two heroic narrative poems, *Venus and Adonis* (1593) and Lucrece (1594). His sonnets were written earliest by 1598 and published in 1609. The sonnets refer cryptically to several persons, among them a handsome young man, a woman called the 'Dark Lady', and a rival poet. Shakespeare's name was also on the title page of *The Passionate Pilgrim* (1599), issued by the publisher William Jaggard. The identity of the brunette, who appreared in Shakespeare's later poems, has been a mystery. According to one theory, she was the Countess of Pembroke. George Bernard Shaw believed she was one of Elizabeth I's ladies-in-waiting, Mary Fritton. Some have thought she was the mother of Shakespeare's supposed illegitimate son, Henry Davenant. Or she might have been Marie Mountjoy, Shakespeare's London landlady, or the black prostitute Luce Morgan, or Emilia Bassano, the daughter of a court musician and mistress of the Lord Chamberlain, Lord Hunsdon. And there is a theory that the Dark Lady was not a "she" at all, but Shakespeare's patron Henry Wriothesley, Earl of Southampton.

JONATHAN SWIFT

(30.11.1667 – 19.10.1745)

Jonathan Swift was an Anglo-Irish poet, writer and cleric who gained reputation as a great political writer and an essayist. Jonathan, who became Dean of St. Patrick's in Dublin, is also known for his excellence in satire. His most remembered works include *Gulliver's Travels, A Modest Proposal, An Argument against Abolishing Christianity* and *A Tale of a Tub.*

Jonathan Swift was born on 30 November, 1667 in Dublin, Ireland, to an Irish father and an English mother. Jonathan, who was the second child and the only son of his parents, was born seven months after his father's death. His mother left him with his father's family and returned to England. After losing his parent's contact, Jonathan stayed with his uncle Godwin, who sent him to Kilkenny College for studies. After completing primary schooling, Jonathan went on to study at the Dublin University in 1682, and received a B.A. degree in 1686. He had to drop his further studies after a political clash broke in Ireland. Jonathan was forced to leave the place and moved to England in 1688, where with the help of his mother, he secured a job as secretary of an English diplomat Sir William Temple at Moor Park.

Swift left Temple in 1690 because of his persisting illness but returned in the next year. It was during this period that he began to show signs of Meniere's disease, which remained until his death. Jonathan received his M.A. degree from the Oxford University in 1692 and left Moor Park and moved to Ireland where he was appointed as a priest in the Church of Ireland. He again returned to Temple in 1696 for ever. Working as an assistant to Temple, he was given many responsibilities such as writing memoirs and correspondence for publication. Swift wrote *The Battle of the Books* in 1690, a satire, which was finally published in 1704. After Temple's death on 27 January 1699, Swift stayed in England for a brief period and returned to Ireland to become Dean of St. Patrick's Cathedral in Dublin.

Swift was awarded Doctor of Divinity from Trinity College, Dublin, in 1702. During this period he wrote *A Tale of Tub* and his previous work *A Battle of Books* was published. With the success of these two, he began to achieve excellence as a writer and came into contact with Alexander Pope, Johan Gay and John Arbuthnot. During the years 1707-1709, Swift remained politically active and again in 1710, he travelled to London seeking the claims of Irish clergy to the First-Fruits and Twentieths.

As his urges to the Whig administration of Lord Godolphin went unheeded, he published a political pamphlet *The Conduct of the Allies* in 1711. The pamphlet harshly criticised the Whig government for its incapability to end the war with France. The Tory government, an opposition party to the Whig government, recruited Swift as editor of The *Examiner* when it came into power in 1710. The party initiated negotiations with France and signed the Treaty of Utrecht in 1713 which ended the War of the Spanish Succession. After the Whig government again returned to power in 1714, the Tory leaders were charged with treason and tried for illegal negotiations with France.

Swift was widely believed to share an intimate and close relationship with a girl Esther Johnson. He first met her when she was eight years old. The two maintained a close but ambiguous relationship for the rest of his life. They were believed to have secretly married, though there is no definite proof corroborating this. But it was certain that she held a special place in his heart throughout his life. In his later life, Swift was linked to another fatherless girl, Esther Vanhomrigh, who presumably was infatuated with him, though Swift later tried to break off relationship with her.

With the Whig government coming to power, Jonathan Swift left England for one more time. He returned to Ireland and began a series of political writing in Irish support. Some of his notable works during this period are *Proposal for Universal Use of Irish Manufacturer* (1720), *Drapier's Letters* (1724) and *A Modest Proposal* (1729). Some of his masterpieces, *Travels into Several Remote Nations of the World* and *Gulliver's Travels* also came during that period. In 1726 he visited England where he stayed with his life long friends Alexander Pope, John Arbuthnot and John Gay. With the help of them, Swift anonymously published his book *Gulliver's Travels* in 1726. The book was proved to be such a huge success that it's French, German and Dutch version had to be published in 1727.

Esther Johnson's death on 28 January 1728 shattered him and pushed him into a state of mental illness. He wrote his book *The Death of Mrs. Johnson* as a tribute to Esther Johnson after her death. Moved by her death, Swift began to write extensively on death and in 1731, he wrote *Verses on the Death of Dr. Swift,* which was published in 1739. Before that in 1738, he had begun to show signs of mental illness and gradually lost his ability to speak and walk. On 19 October 1745 Jonathan Swift died. In accordance to his wishes, he was buried near the grave of Esther Johnson and his assets were donated to found a hospital for the mentally ill.

SIR WALTER SCOTT

Walter Scott was born in Edinburgh, the son of a solicitor Walter Scott and Anne, daughter of a professor of medicine. An early illness - polio - left him lame in the right leg. Six of his 11 brothers and sisters died in infancy. However, Scott grew up to be a man over six feet and great physical endurance.

(05.08.1771 – 21.09.1832)

Scott's interest in the old Border tales and ballads had early been awakened, and he devoted much of his leisure to the exploration of the Border country. In early years Scott spent in Sandy-Know, in the residence of his paternal grandfather. There his grandmother told him tales of old heroes. At the age of eight he returned to Edinburgh. He attended Edinburgh High School (1779-1783) and studied at Edinburgh University arts and law (1783-86, 1789-92). At the age of sixteen he had already started to collect old ballads and later translated into English Gottfried Bürger's ballads *The Wild Huntsman* and *Lenore* and *Goetz of Berlichingen* (1799) from Johann Wolfgang von Goethe's play. Scott was apprenticed to his father in 1786 and in 1792 he was called to the bar. In 1799 he was appointed sheriff deputy of the county of Selkirk. After an unsuccessful love affair with Williamina Belsches of Fettercairn - she married Sir William Forbes - Scott married in 1797 Margaret Charlotte Charpentier (or Charpenter), daughter of Jean Charpentier of Lyon in France. They had five children.

In 1802-03 appeared Scott's first major work, *Minstrels of the Scottish Border*. As a poet Scott rose into fame with the publication of *The Lay of the Last Minstrel* (1805) about an old border country legend. He had burned its first version, when his friends did not like it. Scott returned to the poem in 1802, when a horse had kicked him and he spent three days in bed. *The Lay of the Last Minstrel* became a huge success and made him the most popular author of the day. It was followed by *Marmion* (1808), a historical romance in tetrameter, set in 1813, and concerning the attempts of Lord Marmion to marry the rich Lady Clare.

In 1810 appeared *The Lady in the Lake* and in 1813 *Rokeby.* Scott's last major poem, *The Lord of the Isles,* was published in 1815. Later Thomas Love Peacock (1785-1866) ridiculed in *The Four Ages of Poetry* Scott, Byron, and the Romantic *Lake Poets* Wordsworth and Coleridge: "While the historian and the philosopher are advancing in, and accelerating the progress of knowledge, the poet is wallowing in the rubbish of departed ignorance, and raking up the ashes of dead savages to find gewgaws and rattles for the grown up babies of the age. Mr.Scott digs up the poachers and cattle-stealers of the ancient border. Lord Byron cruizes for thieves and pirates on the shores of Morea and among the Greek Islands. Mr. Southey wades through ponderous volumes of travels and old chronicles..." Verses from *The Lady of the Lake,* including 'Hail to the Chief who in triumph advances!" were put to music by James Sanderson (1769-1841) and became the march traditionally played to honour the President of the United States.

In 1806 Scott became clerk to the Court of Sessions in Edinburgh – this work took only a few hours daily and half of the year he was free. His long holidays Scott spent at Ashestiel, situated on the Tweed River. To increase his income he started a printing and publishing business with his friend James Ballantyne. The firm had in the 1810s financial difficulties, and Scott spent his time in immense labours for his publishers, much of it hack editorial work. Scott also expanded during these years his Abbotsford estate, but it was not until 1826 when the final crash came. He accepted all Ballantyne's debts and decided to pay them off with his writings – the sum was £130,000 (millions today). In his diary he wrote: "I am become a sort of writing automaton, and truly the joints of my knees, especially the left, are so stiff and painful in rising and sitting down, that I can hardly help screaming – I that was so robust and active..."

Difficulties lasted the best of Scott's writing career. To be more productive he used a massive desk with two desktops and kept two projects going at a time. Although Scott's books were sold at prices as high as 31s. 6d., they found much new middle-class readers, and there was no interest in lowering the prices. In comparison, low-cost books, booklets, were offered for the "white-collar" workers at sixpence a piece, and paperbound books were sold for 5 shillings.

Scott's influence as a novelist was profound. He established the form of the historical novel and his work inspired such writers as Bulwer-Lytton, G. Eliot, and the Brontës. In the United States the scholar W.E.B. Du Bois (1868-1963) said in his address in 1926, that he learned most of Scott's *Lady of the Lake* by heart at school, adding: "In after life once it was my privilege to see the lake."

In the 1930s European Marxist critics found Scott again, and interpreted his novels in term of historicism. The most prominent admirer of Scott was the Hungarian philosopher and aesthetician György Lucács. Modernist taste classified Scott to the category of the subliterary or juvenile. "It is impossible to believe that Scott lives anywhere today," wrote Ford Madox Ford in his *The March of Literature* (1938), "he might perhaps in a doctor's dining-room in Marseilles or Tarascon, in a child's nursery in Buenos Aires, or a housemaid's pantry on Boston Hill."

NAGARJUNA

Acharya Nagarjuna is one of the most important figures of early Buddhism. His significance is emphasized by the fact that he is sometimes referred to as the "Second Buddha."

Nagarjuna was a leading voice in the establishment of Mahayana Buddhism, which emphasized the Bodhisattva vow to work for the enlightenment and freedom from suffering of all beings and not merely oneself.

Nagarjuna lived in India in the second century CE, at about the time that Buddhism was being taken to China and other east Asian regions. He was born into a Brahmin family in Bedarwa (The Land of the Palms) in southern India, fulfilling a prophecy attributed to the Buddha:

In the Southern region, in the Land of the Palms,

The monk Shriman of great renown,

Known by the name, 'Naga',

Will destroy the positions of existence and non-existence.

Having proclaimed to the world my vehicle,

The unsurpassed Great Vehicle,

He will accomplish the ground, Very Joyful,

And depart to the Land of Bliss.

As a young boy, Nagarjuna excelled in his studies, showing early signs of his keen intellect, which is reflected in his later writings.

A fascinating story is told of how he came to the Buddhist path. As a young man, Nagarjuna along with three friends, learned the secret of invisibility from a sorcerer. They used this ability to secretly enter the royal palace and seduce the attractive young women at court. The ruse was discovered, and the royal guards were told to attack where they saw footprints appearing without apparent cause. All three of Nagarjuna's friends were killed, and Nagarjuna survived only by staying close to the king.

This experience taught the young Nagarjuna how desires lead to suffering, and he fled to the mountains to become a monk, becoming the student of a Buddhist master.

He later journeyed throughout India, often engaging in theological debate with proponents of various religions, including other Buddhists who opposed the newly emerging Mahayana expression of Buddhism.

Nagarjuna eventually founded a monastery, establishing his own order of monks. Unlike other Buddhist teachers of the time, he taught from his own direct insight, rather than simply restating and recategorizing the sacred literature that had been passed down.

One of Nagarjuna's major contributions to Buddhist literature is the hugely influential *Prajnaparamita Sutras* (Wisdom Discourses), which is a series of conversations between the Buddha and his disciples on the importance of Sunyata (emptiness) in coming to full awakening. The story is told that, one day while meditating near a lake, a naga, or water wisdom snake, came to the surface and asked him to journey to the underwater kingdom of nagas in order to teach them. He did so, and as a gift of thanks, he was entrusted with the twelve-volume *Prajnaparamita Sutras,* which were deemed ready to be released back into human consciousness. This event is also said to be how he came by his name, Nagarjuna.

Another important work associated with Nagarjuna is the *Mulamadhyamaka Karika* ("Verses from the Center" or "Fundamental Wisdom of the Middle Way"), a series of koan-like riddles and inquiries into the emptiness and the ephemeral nature of self-existence in the form of poetry.

In the iconography associated with Nagarjuna, he is often depicted seated in meditation beneath a protective canopy of nagas, the serpents associated with awakened wisdom.

WILLIAM WORDSWORTH

(07.04.1770 – 23.04.1850)

William Wordsworth was one of the greatest English poets who, along with the other poet and friend Samuel Coleridge, ushered into the English Romantic faction with the publication of their joint work *Lyrical Ballads* in 1798. Wordsworth is mainly known for his autobiographical poem 'The Prelude', initially known as 'To Coleridge' - which he expanded many times in his later life, and the work was published posthumously. He also wrote a number of other poems including *The Lucy Poems* and *Poems in Two Volumes* that came in the year 1807. His creations helped launch the Romantic era in English literature and took it to the peak of the art for which he was awarded a civil list pension from the government in his later life. He was also appointed the Poet Laureate of England in 1843.

William Wordsworth was born on 7 April, 1770 in Cumberland, a place in the Lake District of England. He was second of the five children of his father John Wordsworth - who was a legal representative of James Lowther, 1st Earl of Lonsdale, and mother Ann Cookson. Throughout his life, William remained close to his sister Dorothy, who was one year older to him and shared the same passion for nature and poetry. His other siblings were Richard, John and Christopher who became lawyer, poet and researcher respectively. William Wordsworth lost his mother in 1778 at the age of eight and five years later in 1783, he lost his father.

After his mother died, William was sent to Hawkshead Grammar School for his primary education, though he had attended a few low quality schools in Cocker Mouth where he learned little apart from the Bible. At Hawkshead, he met Mary Hutchinson, who would later become his wife. Wordsworth wrote his first sonnet in 1787, which was published in the *European Magazine* and in the same year he enrolled in St. John's College in Cambridge. He was awarded a B.A. degree in 1791, after which he returned to Hawkshead.

In 1793, Wordsworth's first poetry collection was published. Though he had made his debut as a poet and gained remarkable success, his financial condition remained meagre. In 1795, he received a legacy of $ 900 from Raisley Calvert which came as an aid to his hard pressed finance. In the same year, he met another poet Samuel Taylor Coleridge and the two developed a life-long friendship and together they published *Lyrical Ballads* – a collection of romantic poems, in 1798. The collection-which had an equal contribution of Wordsworth and Coleridge - met with remarkable success.

The second edition was published in 1800 with William Wordsworth as its author which inflamed much argument in its third edition in 1802. Fourth and final edition of *Lyrical Ballads* came in 1805. After that William started working on an autobiographical piece that later became known as *The Prelude.* At that time he was living in Germany with his sister Dorothy, where he wrote a number of poems including his famous one *The Lucy Poems*. His most of the works during that period revolved around death, endurance, separation, abandonment and grief which were his own life's reflection.

In his later life, Wordsworth began working on his philosophical poems, which he intended to publish in three parts. In 1807, his *Poems in Two Volumes* was published which gave him further recognition from people. In 1813, Wordsworth was appointed as Distributor of Stamps for Westmorland offering an income of $400 per year. The offer made him financially secure and he moved with his family to Royal Mount in Ambleside in the same year where he lived for the rest of his life.

In 1838, Wordsworth was awarded an honorary Doctor of Civil Law degree from Durham University and he received the same honour from Oxford University in 1839. In 1842, he was awarded a civil list pension from the government which ensured an income of $300 per year. Wordsworth's best reward came in 1843, when he was made the Poet Laureate of England.

William Wordsworth died on 23 April, 1850 and was buried at St. Oswald's Church in Grasmere. His *Poem to Coleridge* was published posthumously as *The Prelude* which is recognized as his one of his best works.

WILLIAM MAKEPEACE THACKERAY

(18.07.1811 – 24.12.1863)

William Makepeace Thackeray was an English author, novelist and satirist who gained international fame and popularity for his novel *Vanity Fair.* His most famous works include the novels *Catherine, The Luck of Barry Lyndon* and *The Adventures of Philip.* Initially started as a satirist and parodist, Thackeray produced some fine examples of this genre. Among them are *Timbuctoo,* published in 1829, and a collection of fictional sketches *The Yellowiplush Papers* published in 1837. The author was also a journalist and columnist and contributed sketches for the *Fraser's Magazine* before writing his first novel. By as early as 1940, Thackeray had gained popularity with the release of his two travel books *The Paris Sketch Book* and *The Irish Sketch Book*. Nevertheless, his most enduring success came in 1847, with the release of the novel *Vanity Fair,* which became his masterpiece and one of his best known works.

William Thackeray was born on 18 July, 1811 in Calcutta, India. His father Richmond Thackeray was a high rank secretary to the board of revenue in the British East India Company. Anne Becher, his mother, was also a secretary writer for the East India Company. At age five, William went on attending his first school St. Helena and then at Charterhouse School, which he loathed in part due to the teasing he was subjected to there. His abhorrence for the school is evident in his later fiction where he chose to call it mockingly a "Slaughterhouse". Upon completion of the initial school, he went on to study at Trinity College, Cambridge, but left it in the middle of the session in 1830. Around this period, he had started writing for the college magazine *The Snob* and *The Gownsman.*

Thackeray courted and on 20 August 1836, married Isabella Gethin Shawe, daughter of Mathew Shawe, a colonel. The marriage forced him to find a viable and stable source of income and he finally got a job with *Fraser's Magazine.* As a journalist, he wrote art criticism alongside contributing sketches. During this period, he produced two fictional works *Catherine* and *The Luck of Barry Lyndon.* He began working for a magazine *Punch,* publishing *The Snob Papers.* The works would later become known as *The Book of Snobs.*

The book gave him initial success and fame, however, the happiness was overshadowed by the growing illness of his wife, who had reached in her last phase of depression. In 1840, he took his wife to Ireland in the hope to improve her condition, though it hardly helped him in the matter. She threw herself into the sea on their way to Ireland and was rescued by the seamen. Two years after in 1842, she was confined in a home in Paris, where she lived until her death in 1893.

By as early as 1840, Thackeray had gained popularity with the release of his two travel books *The Paris Sketch Book* and *The Irish Sketch Book.* His landmark success came in 1847, when the novel *Vanity Fair* was first published and soon became one of his most remembered works. With the stunning success of the novel, Thackeray reached at the peak of his success and produced a number of large novels including *Pendennis, The Newcomers,* and *The History of Henry*

Esmond. In 1849, he suffered from a deadly attack of illness which left him bedridden for months. Despite his ailing health and reduced energy, Thackeray continued lecturing at various universities and seminars.

In 1860, he was made editor of the *Cornhill Magazine,* though he preferred the role of a columnist and continued to contribute his *Roundabout Papers* for the magazine. By this time, his health had worsened and he began showing the similar traits of depression as his wife's, partly motivated by the frustration from his reduced creativity. His over-eating and addiction to black pepper further damaged his digestion and made him a heart patient. On the night of 23 December, 1863, the author attended a dinner party and was found dead in his bedroom the next morning. He was fifty two years old at the time of his death. A funeral was held at Kensington Gardens and he was buried on 29 December at Kensal Green Cemetery.

HARRIET BEECHER STOWE

(14.06.1811 – 01.07.1896)

American writer and philanthropist, best-known for the anti-slavery novel *Uncle Tom's Cabin* (1851-52), Stowe wrote the work in reaction to the Fugitive Slave Act of 1850, which made it illegal to assist an escaped slave. In the story Uncle Tom of the title is bought and sold three times and finally beaten to death by his last owner. The book was quickly translated into 37 languages and it sold in five years over half a million copies in the United States. *Uncle Tom's Cabin* was also among the most popular plays of the 19th century.

Harriet Beecher Stowe was born in Litchfield, Connecticut, on June 14, 1811 into a large family. She had two sisters, Catharine and Mary, one half-sister, Isabella, five brothers, William, Edward, George, Henry Ward, and Charles, and two half-brothers, Thomas and James. Harriet herself was the seventh child of her parents, Lyman and Roxana Beecher. "Wish it had been a boy!" said her father after her birth. Lyman was a controversial Calvinist preacher, who saw himself as a soldier of Christ. Roxana, a granddaughter of General Andrew Ward, died of tuberculosis at 41 – Harriet was four at that time. Two years later a stepmother took over the household.

Stowe was named after her aunt, Harriet Foote, who influenced deeply her thinking, especially with her strong belief in culture. Samuel Foote, her uncle, encouraged her to read works of Lord Byron and Sir Walter Scott. When Stowe was eleven, she entered the seminary at Hartford,

Connecticut, kept by her elder sister Catharine. The school had advanced curriculum and she learned languages, natural and mechanical science, composition, ethics, logic, mathematics - subjects that were generally taught to male students. Four years later she was employed as an assistant teacher. Her father married again - he became the president of Lane Theological Seminary.

Catharine and Harriet founded a new seminary, the Western Female Institute. With her sister Stowe wrote a children's geography book. In 1834 Stowe began her literary career when she won a prize contest of the *Western Monthly Magazine,* and soon Stowe was a regular contributor of stories and essays. Her first book, *The Mayflower,* appeared in 1843. Stowe's fame opened her doors to the national literary magazines. She started to publish her writings in *The Atlantic Monthly* and later in *Independent* and in *Christian Union.* For some time she was the most celebrated woman writer in *The Atlantic Monthly* and in the New England literary clubs. In 1853, 1856, and 1859 Stowe made journeys to Europe, where she became friends with George Eliot, Elisabeth Barrett Browning, and Lady Byron. However, the British public opinion turned against her when she charged Lord Byron with incestuous relations with his half-sister. In *Lady Byrion Vindicated* (1870) she accused him in the writing. The magazine *Atlantic,* where the text first appeared, and Stowe, suffered.

In 1836 Stowe married Calvin Ellis Stowe, a professor at her father's theological seminary. He was a widower; his late wife had been Stowe's friend. The early years of their marriage were marked by poverty. Over the next 14 years Stowe had 7 children. In 1850 Calvin Stowe was offered a professorship at Bowdoin, and they moved to Brunswick,

Maine. In Cincinnati Stowe had come in contact with fugitive slaves. She learned about life in the South from her own visits there and saw how cruel slavery was. In addition the Fugitive Slave Law, passed by Congress in 1850, arose much protest - giving shelter or assistance to an escaped slave became a crime. And finally a personal tragedy, the death of her infant Samuel from cholera, led Stowe to compose her famous novel.

It was first published in the anti-slavery newspaper *The National Era*, from June 1851 to April 1852, and later in book form. The story was to some extent based on true events and the life of Josiah Henson. "I could not control the story, the Lord himself wrote it," Stowe once said. "I was but an instrument in His hands and to Him should be given all the praise." When Abraham Lincoln met the author he joked, "So you're the little woman who wrote the book that started this Great War." *Uncle Tom's Cabin* was smuggled into Russia in Yiddish to evade the czarist censor. Leo Tolstoy praised the work and it remained enormously popular also after the Revolution. After the Civil War the sales of the novel declined. The sentimentality and religiosity of the story was considered a drawback. The first film adaptation was made in 1903. 'Uncle Tom' was used pejoratively, meaning white paternalism and black passivity, undue subservience to white people on the part of black people. In the 1970s *Uncle Tom's Cabin*, with its strong female characters, started to attract the attention of feminist critics, and Stowe's vision found now defenders. However, Tom's passivity was compared to Gandhi's strategy of peaceful resistance.

Stowe's later works did not gain the same popularity as *Uncle Tom's Cabin*. She published novels, studies of social life, essays, and a small volume of religious poems. The

Stowes lived in Hartford in summer and spent their winters in Florida, where they had a luxurious home. *The Pearl of Orr's Island* (1862), *Old-Town Folks* (1869), and *Poganuc People* (1878) were partly based on her husband's childhood reminiscences and are among the first examples of local colour writing in New England. *Poganuc People* was Stowe's last novel. Her mental faculties failed in 1888, two years after the death of her husband. She died on July 1, 1896 in Hartford, Connecticut.

JOHN RUSKIN

(08.02.1819 – 20.01.1900)

John Ruskin was born in London on 8 February 1819. His father was a wine importer who owned a company that later became known as Allied Domecq. The only child of his father, John Ruskin began his education at home and then enrolled into King's College in London. Later he took admission in Christ Church College, Oxford University, to further his studies, where he won the new Digate Prize for his poetry. Though he was never an outstanding performer, the university granted him a voluntary fourth class degree.

John first wrote for an *Architecture Magazine* in 1836-7 which was published as The Poetry of Architecture and soon afterwards, in 1839, his work *The Transactions of the Meteorological Society* was published. His initial work was not of much significance and went unnoticed, before his first major writing *Modern Painters* came in 1843. The work, which was published under an unspecified identity, became promoter of modern landscape painters - specifically J.M.W. Turner, who in Ruskin's opinion, were far greater than several old artists of that era. As an artist, John himself was very close to nature and his painting often revolved around his observation of nature, such as clouds, trees, seas and water. The remark brought him under fire and drew criticism from the people who had discarded Turner's work as "meaningless mess". The remark was taken as an affront to the great artists of that era. However, according to Ruskin-unlike old masters, Turner expressed a more thoughtful knowledge of the truths of nature.

In another controversy, Ruskin was alleged to have destroyed several paintings of Turner, who was a member of the Royal Academy and a friend of John Ruskin, because of their obscene theme. However, recent findings have proved these claims wrong. After working upon nature for some time, John shifted to the subject of architect. His two major writings on the subject were *The Seven Lamps of Architecture* and *The Stones of Venice*, where he strongly viewed that architecture cannot be separated from integrity. These writings were published in his name and became his road to fame.

In 1885, John Ruskin established the School of Art in Sidney Street, Cambridge, which later became known as Anglia Ruskin University. Meanwhile, he continued to write critical reviews of the art work exhibited every year. He advocated the Gothic style for modern culture and urged architects to adopt the same. He had great respect for old buildings and he strongly advocated the conservation of the ancient buildings.

A fervent critic, Ruskin renounced art criticism in the later years of 1850s and embarked upon commentary on politics. His idea of socialism matured during this period and he gave away most of his assets after his father's death as he believed that a rich person cannot be a socialist. In 1870, he established a charity Guild of St George and supported it with his art collection worth millions. During this period, he was visiting faculty and became the first Slade Professor of Fine Arts in 1869 at the Working Men's College, London.

Ruskin's outlook in socialism played a key role in the growth of Christian Socialism. He believed that the best deserves first. That is, the employment system should be such that the only best worker gets employed first, rather than one who offers to do the work at half the rate. He endorsed the fixed wage system, which, in his opinion sustains the quality work and promotes a healthy competition.

In his later life, Ruskin continued writing contemptuous reviews and articles that often made him face legal consequences. In one of such cases, he was sued by James McNeill Whistler in 1878. Though he was ordered to pay only a small amount as compensation, Ruskin's reputation was badly affected after the incident.

During the Aesthetic movement and Impressionism, Ruskin estranged from the modern art world and began writing on other issues and continuing to support humanitarian movements, such as Home Arts and Industries Association. In his later life, Ruskin lived in Brantwood, a house on the shores of Coniston, where the Ruskin Museum was established in 1901 after his death on 20 January, 1900.

WALT WHITMAN

(31.05.1819 – 26.03.1892)

Walter Whitman was an American poet, journalist and humanist. The poet is mainly known for his approach to Transcendentalism and realism and mastery in free verses, which would mirror in his works. Among his most famous works, is his poetry collection *Leaves of Grass,* which was also his first significant work as a poet. The collection was first published in 1855 and since then, he kept it revising and expanding until his death. The poetry was initially labelled and banned for its obscenity though it later gained popularity and has been translated into a number of foreign languages. Whitman was also a teacher and a government clerk before taking on writing and worked as a nurse during the American Civil War. Though he opposed the slavery system in America and wrote poetry moved by their sufferings, he did not participate in the abolitionary movement at any point in his life. The poet died in 1892 at age seventy two.

Walt Whitman was born on 31 May, 1819 in Long Island. New York, and was the second of nine children born to his parents Walter and Louisa Van Velsor Whitman. His childhood was not a happy one and was raised amidst a hard pressed finance of his family. They kept on moving from one place to another, which was also due to the bad economic conditions and he took up his first employment of many, as early as at the age of eleven. He was hired as an office boy of two lawyers and later as an apprentice. He was then employed by the newspaper *The Patriot,* where he learned about the printing press and typesetting. His family moved to West Hills leaving him behind, and he continued to work for another printer Alden Spooner, editor of the weekly newspaper the *Long-Island Star*. By this time, he had begun reading avidly, became a patron of a library and joined various debating societies. He also began writing poetry during this period, which were anonymously published in the *New York Mirror.*

In 1836, Whitman joined the family in Hempstead where he taught at various schools for the next two years. Though he was never happy with the job and finally left it, moving back to New York seeking to set up his newspaper, *The Long Islander.* After working there for a few months, he sold the publication to another publisher and joined the *Long Island Democrat* as a typesetter. He once again turned back to teaching and published a series of ten editorials 'Sun Down Papers–From the Desk of a Schoolmaster'. In 1842, he became editor of the *Brooklyn Eagle.*

Whitman claimed poems to be his first love and regardless of the job he was in, continued to write poetry in his early years which gave him initial success. During the 1850s, he embarked upon writing *Leaves of Grass,* his first work that would bring him his greatest success. The collection was published with his own money in 1855. It was published anonymously and raised much interest within a short span of time. Critics called the poetry as obscene, profane and harshly criticized it for its sexual theme; however, some praised it for its ingenious use of free verses. Ralph Waldo Emerson was one of them. With Emerson coming for his support, the selling of the book was raised considerably and the second edition of it was published in 1856. Since then, Whitman continued to revise and expand the collection until his death. On 11 July 1855, Whitman's father Walt died at age sixty five. The verses brought him both fame and controversies, though financial success still eluded him and he had to get back to his journalism work. In 1857, he joined the Brooklyn's *Daily Times,* where he contributed as its editor and writer until 1859.

With the onset of the American Civil War, Whitman wrote his poem 'Beat! Beat! Drums', that appeared as a call for the country. Whitman's brother George's involvement in the war as a soldier worried him as the news of mass killings kept coming in and he rushed to south to find him. On his way to south, Whitman witnessed and had a close experience of the pain and sufferings of the soldiers. Though luckily he found his brother well and alive, the violence and killing of the war had moved him so much that he decided to leave New York for good and left for Washington in 1862. In Washington, Whitman took up a part time job in the army paymaster's office and became a nurse to those injured in the war. He would recall the experience in *The Great Army of the Sick,* published in 1863.

In 1864, Whitman's brother George was taken into custody by the Confederates in Virginia and another brother Andrew Jackson succumbed to death from tuberculosis. After a difficult end of the year 1864, Whitman succeeded in receiving a government job in the Bureau of Indian Affairs in the Department of the Interior in 1865, though he was fired as soon as his identity as the author of the blasphemous book *Leaves of Grass* was found by the secretary. In 1865, George was released and granted a pardon because of his failing health. O'Connor, a friend of him, went enraged at the news of his firing from the job and published a biographical study of Whitman called *The Good Gray Poet* in 1866. Whitman's reputation was further restored with the release of his poem 'O Captain! My Captain'!, a poem to Abraham Lincoln. In 1868, *Poems of Walt Whitman* was published in England.

Whitman as a poet used symbolic style in his poetry and his works seemingly were fascinated with the subject of death and sexuality. Abandoning the conventional prose-like poetic form, he exuded his mastery in the free verses for which he is called as the 'Father of Free Verse'. His works are considered as a mirror to his country America, as he accentuated the connection between a poet and its country. His works are also influenced by and draw heavily upon his belief in deism.

As early as in 1873, Whitman suffered from a paralytic stroke. His mother, to whom he had been unusually close, passed away in the same year. Depressed and broken, Whitman moved to New Jersey to be with his brother George and lived there until he found a home in 1884. Meanwhile, Whitman released more editions of *Leaves of Grass,* publishing in 1876, 1881 and 1889. He produced a further edition of the book, which was to be its last, in 1891. During this period, he became obsessed with the frequent thoughts of death, and often wrote of his pain and suffering in his notebook. He also bought a mausoleum-shaped house in his last days. Walt Whitman died on 26 March, 1892 of bronchial pneumonia. A grand funeral was held and his body was buried in his tomb at Harleigh Cemetery, where remains of his parents and brothers were moved with him.

GEORGE ELIOT

(22.11.1819 – 22.12.1880)

Mary Anne Evans was born on 22 November, 1819, in Arbury, Warwickshire, England, in a farmer, family. She was the third child of her parents Robert Evans, a local farmer, and Christina Evans and had two surviving full siblings, Chrissey and Issac. Mary Anne, better known as Marian, was a brilliant student and an avid reader and took keen interest in literature as a child. She received her primary education from boarding schools in Attleborough, Nuneaton and Coventry, where she met her lifelong mentor Maria Lewis. One of the significant influences on her early life is religion and her early religious beliefs are marked by confusion and doubts about the Christianity which will plague her throughout her life. As a child, she wrote poetry and fiction and was admired for her skills at writing.

After the death of her mother in 1839, she left the school and returned home to take care of her father. Meanwhile, she continued her education with the help of a private tutor and Maria Lewis. After her brother Issac married and took over the house they were living in, Marian and her father moved to Foleshill in Coventry in 1841. The new place widened her social circle and she formed strong friendship with people that will last forever. One of the most influential associations he formed there was with the Brays, Charles Bray and Cara Bray. Charles Bray was a wealthy businessman and a philanthropic, who shared the same religious views with Marian.

In a society of liberal theology, she began to form atheistic beliefs and deeply doubted the Biblical stories. Such thoughts were corroborated by the people she met there and in 1942, she stopped going to church, to her father's dismay. However, she began to attend church with respect when her father stopped talking to her, the relationship between the father and daughter remained restrained after that. Her father died after an extended illness in 1849. Meanwhile she had started working on her first major work that was the translation of David Strauss' *Life of Jesus,* which she completed in 1846.

After her father's death, Marian went on a tour to Switzerland with the Bray couple and decided to live alone in Geneva instead of returning home. However, she returned to England in 1850 and made up her mind to move to London with the hope to become a writer. There she came in contact with John Chapman, a London publisher and bookseller. Impressed with her translation of Strauss, he asked her to contribute articles and essays for the *Westminster Review.* She became the assistant editor of the magazine in 1858. For the next few years, Marian took up lodgings in Chapman's house where he lived with his wife and mistress.

While working with the *Westminster Review,* she had become increasingly popular in a male dominating literary world of London, where it was not conventional and usual to mix with the male dominated society of London. By that time, Marian Evans had begun to use 'George Eliot' as her pen name. George Henry proved to be a very supportive person and became her pillar of strength until his death. He encouraged Eliot – who was still contributing pieces to the Westminster Review – to try her hand at fiction writing. With his unwavering support and faith in her ability, she completed the first *Scenes of Clerical Life* in 1858, which was first published in *Blackwood's Magazine* around that year. The book was a huge success and became her most acclaimed work.

In 1859, she completed her first novel *Adam Bede* which was published under an anonymous identity in 1859. The novel raised much curiosity among the people as to who the author was. Finally, when the secret could not be kept any longer, George Eliot admitted to the authorship of the book. The book, which revealed many stunning facts about her private life, came as a shock to her readers, though it did not affect her popularity among her admirers. She continued to work upon her next bestselling novel *The Mill on the Floss* which was published in the following year. It was much before the couple's relationship was accepted in the society.

She began to work another novel *Middlemarch* in 1869, which was finally printed in 1871. The record-breaking sell of this novel made her much famous and richer that she was often called 'the greatest living English novelist'. The huge success made people forget about her private affairs and so-called 'unlawful' relationship with Henry. She continued working and wrote her last novel *Daniel Deronda* which was published in 1876 and the Lewes moved to Witley in Surrey. Here she met her tragic fate in 1878, when her lifelong partner and supporter George Henry died after a long illness living her alone and depressed.

Now sixty, Marian was old and ill and had been suffering from kidney disease for years. It was less than one year after her marriage that she fell ill with a serious throat infection. Fate once again made a cruel decision and she died just after seven months of her marriage on 22 December, 1880. She was buried next to her spiritual husband George Lewes in Highgate Cemetery in London.

LEO TOLSTOY

(28.08.1828 – 20.11.1910)

Leo Tolstoy was a Russia-born writer and poet and is regarded as the world's greatest poet and novelist. One of the legacies of the poet is the culmination of the Realist Fiction that he achieved with the publication of his two masterpieces *War and Peace* and *Anna Karenina.* In his later life, Leo explored many talents and emerged as an essayist, education reformer and an excellent dramatist, and gained reverence as the most influential member of the noble Tolstoy family. His ideas on non-violence made him a devoted Christian Anarchist and pacifist and he renounced the authority of Orthodox Church in 1901. Though he never called himself an anarchist, his later teachings can be classified as Christian Anarchism. His much acclaimed book *The Kingdom of God is Within You,* which came out in 1893, is a mirror of his religious and ethical teachings.

Leo Tolstoy was born on 28 August, 1828, at Yasnaya Polyana in Central Russia in a noble Russian family. He was the fourth child of Maria Volkonsky and Nicolay Ilvich Tolstoy. His mother died when he was two. Tolstoy further lost his father at the age of nine and went on to stay with his aunt Madame Ergolsky. In 1844, he enrolled into Kazan University to study Turco-Arabic literature, but dropped out in the middle of a term in 1847. According to his autobiography, he was frustrated and committed every crime of drinking, gambling and visiting brothels in his pursuit for pleasure. Addicted to gambling, he had to sell out most of his father's inheritance.

He returned to his birth place at Yasnaya Polyana in the hope to educate and help the peasants working in his estates. It did not amuse him for long and in 1851 he accompanied his elder brother Nikolay to Chechnya to join the military service where he joined an artillery unit battalion as a volunteer of private rank. While serving in the army, Tolstoy began writing short stories and faced several rejections before his first novel *Childhood* was published in 1852. The book proved to be an immediate success and catapulted him in the front row of Russian writers. Encouraged by the success of *Childhood,* which was a reflection of his own childhood, he continued with *Boyhood and Youth.* He further wrote the battlefield observation based on his experience in the army.

With his growing success as a writer, Tolstoy became a renowned name in the literary world. He left army in 1855 and between the years 1856-1861, he travelled to many foreign countries. In 1857, he again travelled to European countries and wrote his experience there in his books *Lucerne and Three Deaths* and *Kholstomer.* During this period he emerged as an education reformer and in 1859, Tolstoy established a school for peasants' children at Yasnaya. He also wrote several stories for them and took a keen interest in teaching these unprivileged people.

However, a turning point came in his life when his elder brother died on 20 September 1860, which shattered him. Tolstoy described the incident as devastating and his first encounter with the preordained reality of death. Deeply disturbed by his brother's death, Tolstoy began to lose his mental stability and often confessed his remorse in his personal diary. This state continued for at least one year till 1861. After getting over his shock and grief, Tolstoy accepted the honorary post of Justice of the Peace in 1861.

Tolstoy began to write his masterpiece *War and Peace* in 1862 and six volumes of the book were published between the year 1863 and 1869. He started his next classic *Anna Karenina* in 1873, which was a reflection of his own married life, and was first published in the *Russian Herald* in 1876. Throughout his life, Tolstoy felt an insatiable thirst for a realistic and moral justification of life and it remained the centre of his literary works. During this period he experienced his deepest fear of self-questioning and self-criticising as father and husband.

He harshly disparaged himself for his egoistical concerns and self-interest. These thoughts left him in depths of despair and a state of moral crisis. Overwhelmed by the bouts of remorse and grief upon his previous life, he wrote his *Confession* in 1879. He further wrote a number of books, criticizing the Orthodox Church and government. Moving on to philosophical and spiritual topics, he authored books such as *A Criticism of Dogmatic Theology* (1880), *A Short Exposition of the Gospels* (1881), *What I Believe* (1882), and *What Then Must We Do?* (1886).

In his later life, Tolstoy preached non-violence, vegetarianism and chastity. He himself gave up meat, alcohol and tobacco, and embraced the teaching of Jesus. His book *The Kingdom of God is Within You* which came in 1893, is a mirror of his religious and ethical teachings. Tolstoy renounced the authority of Orthodox Church in 1901, and though he never called himself an anarchist, his later teachings can be classified as Christian Anarchism.

By this time, he had become increasingly interested in the subject of life and death and authored books such as *How Much Land Does a Man Need, War and Peace* and *Kholstomer,* examining the complexity of relationship between life and death. After his excommunication in 1901, he became known as a Christian Anarchist, and his teachings were somehow related to communism. As his reputation grew immensely, he began to attract followers from across the country and people began to preach Tolstoy's religious doctrines known as 'Tolstoyism'.

LEWIS CARROLL

(27.01.1832–14.01.1898)

Lewis Carroll was born Charles Lutwidge Dodgson at Daresbury in Chesire, England. His father, the Reverend Charles Dodgson, was at that time Curate of the parish. In 1827 he had married his first cousin Frances Jane Lutwidge, Charles was their third child. Dodgson attended a Yorkshire grammar school and Rugby. At Christ Church, Oxford, he studied mathematics and worked from 1855 to 1881 as a lecturer. Dodgson's career in education was troubled by a bad stammer. He lectured and taught with difficulty and he also preached but only occasionally after his ordination in 1861. "The hesitation, from which I have suffered all my life," Dodgson wrote in a letter, "is always worse in reading (when I can see difficult words before they come) than in speaking."

According to anecdotes, Dodgson was very shy and he even hid his hands continually within a pair of gray-and-black gloves. In 1867 he travelled with his friend and colleague Henry Parry Liddon to Russia, where they visited churches, museums and other places of interest. After this journey, he never again left Britain. Dodgson died on January 14, 1898. He was buried in Guilford Cemetery.

In spite of his stammer, Dodgson spoke easily with children, whom he often photographed, first with their clothes on. From July 1866, Dodgson began to take nude photographs, always with the permission of parents. During the next thirteen years, Dodgson took many nude studies, but before he died, he destroyed most the negatives and prints. Dodgson was careful not to show them to anybody, stating in a letter that "there is really no friend to whom I should wish to give photographs which so entirely defy conventional rules."

The sequel *Through the Looking Class* appeared in 1871. It is perhaps more often quoted than the first, featuring the poems 'Jabberwocky' and 'The Walrus' and the 'Carpenter'. The artist John Tenniel refused to illustrate one chapter in *Through the Looking Class* because he thought that it was ridiculous. The chapter was published later in 1872 as 'The Wasp in a Wig'. Dodgson himself always wished to be an artist and as a boy he illustrated all the manuscript magazines, which he made for his younger brothers and sisters. Dodgson's original drawings for *Alice's Adventures Underground* were published in 1961.

The author's life and work has become a constant area for speculation and his exploring of the boundaries of sense and nonsense has inspired a number of psychological studies and novels - and perhaps also the famous English philosopher Ludwig Wittgenstein. The humour of Joseph Heller's famous war novel *Catch-22* (1961) is much in debt to Dodgson. In *Catch-22* the story centres on the USAF regulation, which suggests that willingness to fly dangerous combat missions must be considered insane, but if the airmen seek to be relieved on grounds of mental reasons, the request proves their sanity. The same laws dominate the Wonderland: "'Oh, you can't help that,' said the Cat: 'we're all mad here. I'm mad. You're mad.' 'How do you know I'm mad?' said Alice. 'You must be,' said the Cat, 'or you wouldn't have come here.'"

At the time of their publication, Alice's adventures were considered children's literature, but now Dodgson's stories are generally viewed in a different light. His work has fascinated such critics as Edmund Wilson and W.H. Auden, and logicians and scientist such as Alfred North Whitehead and Bertrand Russell. Virginia Woolf remarked, "The two Alices are not books for children; they are the only books in which we become children."

In the 1960s rock musicians and hippies were attracted to the surrealistic world of *Wonderland,* which inspired such songs as Jefferson Airplane's 'White Rabbit' and The Beatles's 'I am a Walrus'. Fredric Brown used Lewis Carroll's characters and lyrics in his novel *Night of the Jabberwock* (1950). In the 1990s Jeff Noon continued Alice's adventures in *Automated Alice,* in which she is transported to the modern world.

MARK TWAIN

(30.11.1835 – 21.04.1990)

Samuel Langhorne Clemens, better known by his pen name Mark Twain, was an American author, essayist, lecturer and humorist who wrote a series of famous books including *Adventures of Huckleberry Finn* and *The Adventures of Tom Sawyer*. Mark's first important work, *The Celebrated Jumping Frog of Calaveras County* was first published in the *New York Saturday Press* and became a bestseller within a short time. He also wrote a series of travelogues including the bestselling *The Innocents Abroad* - that came in 1869 - and notable short stories such as *Advice for Little Girls* and *The Celebrated Jumping Frogs of Calaveras County* which earned him the worldwide fame and appreciation as a writer. Most of all, the author is known for his notable and insightful satires that gained him reverence from both critics as well as his contemporaries who call him the 'father of the English literature'.

Samuel Langhorne Clemens was born on November 30, 1835 in Florida, Missouri, in the United States. He was the sixth of seven children of his father, a country merchant John Marshall Clemens, and mother Jane Lampton Clemens, and only three of his siblings could survive into their adulthood. At age four, Mark along with his family, moved to a port town Hannibal, situated on the bank of world's second largest river Mississippi.

Mark's father John Clemens died of pneumonia in 1847, and the family was left in financial upheaval. An eleven year old Mark took a job of typesetter in 1851, to aid the family during its hard pressed finance and began contributing articles and humorous sketches for the *Hannibal Journal,* a newspaper run by his brother Orion. At age 18, Mark Twain left this job and became a printer in New York City. As a child, Mark Twain received no formal schooling, but a keen learner, he widened his circle of knowledge by finding information in public libraries. It was his travelling to New Orleans in 1857, that he grew immensely fascinated with the steamboats and became an apprentice cub river pilot, earning his license in 1858. While working as a successful river pilot, he developed a huge attachment for the river, which would become a subject of his books in later life. He lost his brother Henry in 1858, who was also working with him on the boat.

Mark Twain first met Olivia Livy Langdon in 1868 and they married after two years in February 1870. The marriage proved to be contributing towards his career and he met many writers and socialists through his wife, who came from a wealthy but liberal family. The couple settled in Buffalo in New York for sometime where he became an editor in the *Buffalo Express.* Here their first child, a son, was born who died of diphtheria at 19 months. In 1871, they moved to Hartford, Connecticut, where Olivia gave birth to three daughters: Susy, Clara and Jean. Only Clara could survive her twenties and lived to the age of eighty eight.

Twain as a writer initiated with humorous and light verse but embarked on more serious and harsh subjects in his later career. His one of the important works in this category was *Huckleberry Finn,* which combined humor and social criticism. Aside from this, he wrote several travelogues and lectures. *A Tramp Abroad* (1880), his first travelogue and a satirical account of his travels to Germany, Italy and the

Alps, was a sequel to his early work *Innocent Abroad* and was next followed by *The Prince and the Pauper* in 1882. Mark wrote his first important work, *The Celebrated Jumping Frog of Calaveras County* in year 1865, which became a bestseller. Yet many of his works were suppressed, censored or banned in America for various reasons. In 1888, Mark Twain was awarded the Master of Arts degree from Yale University.

Towards the end of his life, Mark Twain travelled and lectured actively. During this period he lost money in many bad investment schemes like mining and printing machines, thus acquiring a huge debt. In 1895, he set off on a world tour to Australia, Canada, India and New Zealand, and only returned when he was able to pay off the debt. Though he suffered from many losses in his personal life, he never lost his sense of humor and talent as a writer. Meanwhile, he had written the famous series *Tom Sawyer Abroad* in 1894 followed by *Tom Sawyer, Detective* in 1896. Mark suffered from yet another emotional setback when his daughter Susy died of meningitis in 1896. Olivia's death in 1904 and Jean's death in 1909 further deepened his pain and left him in the depths of despair.

Mark Twain died of a heart attack on 21 April, 1910 in Redding in Connecticut and now rests at the Woodlawn Cemetery in Elmira, New York, where his wife and other children were buried. He was survived by his daughter Clara.

BANKIM CHANDRA CHATTERJEE

(27.06.1838 – 08.04.1894)

Bankim Chandra Chatterjee was born on June 27, 1838, in the village Kantalpara of the 24 Paraganas district of Bengal. He belonged to a family of Brahmins. The word 'Bankim Chandra' in Bengali means 'the moon on the second day of the bright fortnight'. Bankim Chandra's father Yadav Chandra Chattopadhyaya was in government service. After his birth he was posted to Midnapur as Deputy Collector. He did for Bengali fiction what Michael Madhusudan Dutt had done for Bengali poetry, that is, he brought in imagination.

Chatterjee was more fortunate than Dutt as he did not have to set up his own diction from the very start. The prose style was already standardized; what Chatterjee did was to break its monotony, shear off its ponderous verbosity and give it a twist of informality and intimacy. Chatterjee's own style grew up as he went on writing.

Chatterjee, following the discipline of Isvarchandra Gupta, began his literary career as a writer of verse. Fortunately, he was not slow to feel that poetry was not his metier. He then turned to fiction. His first attempt was a novel in Bengali submitted for a declared prize. The prize did not come to him and the novelette was never published. His first fiction to appear in print was *Rajmohan's Wife*. It was written in English and was probably a translation of the novelette submitted for the prize. *Durgeshnandini,* his first

Bengali romance, was published in 1865. The next novel *Kapalkundala* (1866) is one of the best romances written by Chatterjee. The theme is lyrical and gripping and, in spite of the melodrama and the dual story, the execution is skilful. The heroine, named after the mendicant woman in Bhavabhuti's *Malatimadhava,* is modelled partly after Kalidasa's *Shakuntala* and partly after Shakespeare's Miranda.

The next romance *Mrinalini* (1869) indicates an ameturishness and a definite falling off from the standard. It is a love romance against a historical background sadly neglected and confused. After this Chatterjee was not content to continue only as a writer of prose romances, but appeared also as a writer with the definite mission of stimulating the intellect of the Bengali-speaking people through literary campaign and of bringing about a cultural revival thereby. With this end in view he brought out the monthly *Bangadarshan* in 1872. In the pages of this magazine all his writings, except the very last two works, first came out. These writings include novels, stories, humorous sketches, historical and miscellaneous essays, informative articles, religious discourses, literary criticisms and reviews. *Vishbriksha* (The Poison Tree, 1873) was his first novel to appear serially in *Bangadarshan.*

Chatterjee's next major novel was *Chandrasekhar* (1877) which suffers markedly from the impact of two parallel plots which have little common ground. The scene is once shifted back to eighteenth century. But the novel is not historical. The plot has suffered from the author's weakness for the occult. The next novel *Rajani* (1877) followed the autobiographical technique of Wilkie Collins' *A Woman in White.* The title role was modelled after Bulwar Lytton's Nydia in *The Last Days of Pompeii.* In this romance of a blind girl, Chatterjee is at his best as a literary artist. In

Krishnakanter Will, 1878, Chatterjee added some amount of feeling to imagination, and as a result it approaches nearest to the western novel. The plot is somewhat akin to that of *Poison Tree.*

The only novel of Chatterjee's that can claim full recognition as historical fiction is *Rajsimha* (1881, rewritten and enlarged 1893). *Anandamath* (The Mission House of the Anandas, 1882) is a political novel without a sufficient plot. It definitely marks the decline of Chatterjee's power as a novelist. The plot of the meagre story is based on the Sannyasi rebellion that occurred in North Bengal in 1773. As fiction it can not be called an outstanding work. But as the book that interpreted and illustrated the gospel of patriotism and gave Bengal the song "Bande Mataram" (I worship mother) which became the mantra of nationalism and the national song. Incidentally, it gave tremendous impetus to the various patriotic and national activities culminating in the terrorist movement initiated in Bengal in the first decade of the twentieth century.

Devi Chaudhurani by Chatterjee was published in 1884. The story is romantic and interesting and delightfully told, no doubt. Chatterjee's last novel *Sitaram* (1886) has for its theme the insurgence of a Hindu chief of lower central Bengal against the impotent Muslim rule. The central figure is well delineated but the other figures are either too idealistic or impalpable.

After the novels, the humorous sketches are the outstanding productions of Chatterjee. *Kamalakanter Daptar* (The Scribbling of Kamalakanta, 1875; enlarged as *Kamalakanta,* 1885) contains half humorous and half serious sketches somewhat after De Quincey's *Confessions of an English Opium-eater.* It shows the writer at his best.

Bankim Chandra Chatterjee was a superb story-teller, and a master of romance. He is also a great novelist in spite of the fact that his outlook on life was neither deep nor critical, nor was his canvas wide. But he was something more than a great novelist. He was a pathfinder and a pathmaker. Chatterjee represented the English-educated Bengali with a tolerably peaceful home life, sufficient wherewithal and some prestige, as the bearer of the torch of western enlightment. No Bengali writer before or since has enjoyed such spontaneous and universal popularity as Chatterjee. His novels have been translated in almost all the major languages of India, and have helped to stimulate literary impulses in those languages.

THOMAS HARDY

(02.06.1840 – 11.01.1928)

Thomas Hardy was an English author, novelist and poet, who is mainly known for his contribution in the naturalist movement. Though he always regarded himself as a poet and claimed poems as his first love, they are not as popular as novels composed by him. Hardy's huge popularity lies in the large volume of work, together known as the Wessex stories. These novels, plotted in a semi-fictional place, Wessex, outline the lives of people struggling against their passion and the adverse conditions. Most of his works reflect his stoical glumness and sense of cataclysm in human life. As both poet and author, Hardy displayed his mastery in dealing with themes of disappointment in love and life, human suffering and all-powerful fate. Most of his works are set in the milieu of social tragedy, injustice and evil laws and often have a fatalistic end, with many of the characters falling prey to the unanticipated conditions. Among his most important works are novels *Far from the Madding Crowd, The Return of the Native, Wessex Tales* and *A Pair of Blue Eyes.*

Hardy as a writer is mainly known for his novels. His first novel, *The Poor Man and the Lady* was written in 1867 and was destroyed when the manuscript was refused publication from a number of publishing houses. After a turbulent first experience, Hardy anonymously published two novels *Desperate Remedies* and *Under the Greenwood Tree* in 1871 and 1872 respectively. His first success as a writer came in 1873, with the release of his first important work

A Pair of Blue Eyes. The book was a recollection of his courtship with his first wife Emma.

There are strong suggestions that Hardy's stance on religion swayed between agnosticism and atheism. Most of his works draw heavily upon the strength of all-powerful fate and question the existence of God in the times of human suffering. As an author and poet, Hardy seemingly was fascinated with fatalistic ends and expressed pessimism that was impassive, indifferent. His own life was marked by a religious view that was a mixture of philosophy and spiritualism which did not discard the existence of God, yet questioned it. Hardy rather showed an interest in writing about external supernatural forces, and fascination with ghosts and spirits. However, a Church devotee, Hardy drew heavily upon the role of God in the irony and tragedy of life and human suffering.

Another stunning success was the beginning of the series of *Wessex Tales* which was published after his second novel *Far from the Madding Crowd.* The novel was first published in 1874 and brought him instant success. He next wrote *The Return of the Native,* published in 1878. Hardy moved with his wife to Max Gate, in a house designed by him where he wrote *The Mayor of Casterbridge,* published in 1886 followed by *The Woodlanders* (1887) and *Tess of the d'Urbervilles* (1891).

Hardy's first volume of poetry, *Wessex Poems* was published in 1898. Since then, a prodigious output of his poems was published till 1928. Originally wanting to be a poet, Hardy claimed poem as his first priority, though he could not achieve anything of distinction in this genre and it remained overshadowed by his works in prose. Hardy as a poet showed a sharp observation of his surroundings and nature and wrote poems that displayed his affection for natural world. Although like his novels, his poems also carry the strain of the irony of life, cruel fate and regrets.

Hardy's short stories and novel series are best remembered for their meticulous portrayal of life troubled by social evils, human suffering and struggle against injustice and ill-comprehended laws. Most of his novels are set in a semi-fictional place Wessex, a large area of south-west England. His most controversial novel, *Jude the Obscure* highlights the prejudice and hypocrisy of Victorian society on sexual conduct. In another book *Town on a Tower,* Hardy displays a firm stand against an orthodox and conventional path for attaining love. Fate plays an important role in most of his books and remains the centre of most of his works. His characters always find themselves trapped and are often defeated by the fate and unforeseen conditions. His books portray people fighting against the cruelty of life, injustice and badly framed laws that constrain the social growth.

In December 1927, Hardy fell sick with pleurisy and eventually died in January, 1928. After the funeral on 16 January, he was buried with his first wife Emma and ashes in Poet's Corner.

ELLA WHEELER WILCOX

(05.11.1850 – 30.10.1919)

Ella Wheeler Wilcox's prolific excellence lay in her positive approach and optimistic nature. She had started penning down poetry from an early age and continued to do so till her death. Her poems reflected her optimism - her belief that hope would triumph over despair and good would overcome evil. For Wilcox, the severity and roughness of life did not exist. Wilcox also was a strong believer of reincarnation. She believed that the negativity that life presented was just an opportunity for man to turn into a blessing. Wilcox played part in the establishment of the American Rosicrucian movement and was also appointed as its first Supreme Council officer. Her term as the Supreme Council officer lasted until her death.

Born in the year 1850, on a farm in rural Johnstown, Wisconsin, Ella Wheeler Wilcox was the youngest amongst four siblings. Her mother, Ms. Wilcox, believed in pre-natal influences. According to her, parents could influence the soul personality of their would-be child by their thoughts and ideals and the kid, in his/her later years, would reflect them. When Ella was in her womb, Ms. Wilcox wanted a girl child, who would go on to become a writer. She did not have to wait too long to fulfil her dreams.

Ella Wheeler Wilcox, right from a very tender age, reflected a knack for creative writing. When she was only 8 years old, she wrote her first poem and rhyme. Six years later, at the age of 14, a piece of her prose was published in the *New York Mercury*. She became the pride of her parents and neighbours. However, the feeling of pride was soon swayed away, when Wilcox scored extremely low in mathematics. Though Wilcox came from a not-so-sound financial background, she was enrolled in Madison University.

Eventually, Wilcox left her studies and started pursuing her passion for writing. Just like other writers, she also struggled at the start of her writing career. Though Wilcox would pen down poems, only a few of them would get published, as there were not many potential buyers for her poetry. However, she was not the one to be disheartened by the struggle. She remained optimistic and continued sending her poems to one publisher after the other, with the hope that at least one of them would publish them.

Gradually, Wilcox started living her mother's dream - her poems were being published and she was being recognised. She started making a living out of her work. Her poetry was focused on humanity's spirit and on themes of reincarnation. Her poems had a positive approach. For Wilcox, her poetry was a medium by which she could raise someone's spirit, after his/her death. Her poems gave strength to those who were bereaving for the dead. Wilcox was a strong believer in reincarnation and said that every good thing that one does would get repaid, if not in this life, then in the next. She gave hope in despair and echoed the triumph of the human spirit in every poem she wrote.

At the age of 28, Ella Wheeler Wilcox married Robert Wilcox. He possessed a fine sense of humour and was an Inspiration to her. More than anything, he loved her and her work. The couple was blessed with a son, but he died as an infant. After about 30 years of successful marriage, Robert

Wilcox died in 1916. The couple had promised each other that whoever went first through death would return and communicate with the other. Sad and heartbroken, Wilcox waited for a long time to receive any communication from her beloved and got even more depressed when she heard nothing from him.

Diagnosed with cancer, Ella Wheeler Wilcox died in the year 1919. At the time of her death, she was just a week short of celebrating her 69th birthday.

ARTHUR CONAN DOYLE

(25.05.1859 – 07.07.1930)

Arthur Ignatius Conan Doyle was a Scottish doctor, author and poet, and is most notably remembered for his stories about the detective Sherlock Holmes. Regarded as the leading light of crime and science fiction, the author is best known for the world popular character Sherlock Holmes and the adventures of Professor Challenger. Arthur Doyle was a prolific writer and produced a prodigious output in a variety of genres ranging from science fiction to historical novels to plays and romances and non-fiction stories. The world famous character of detective Sherlock Holmes first appeared in his novel *A Study in Scarlet* in 1887, and from then on Arthur began writing stories starring the character which resulted in about fifty five more Sherlock Holmes stories and four novels starring him.

He wrote many fiction and non-fiction works including *The Stark Munro Letters, The Exploits of Brigadier Gerad, The Hound of the Baskervilles* and his masterpiece *The Lost World.* Many of his works are still in print and have been published in a number of foreign languages.

Born on 22 May, 1859, Arthur Conan Doyle was the son of an English father Charles Altamont Doyle and an Irish mother Nee Mary Foley. His father Charles was a fervent alcoholic and would lead a problematic life amid addiction and depression and eventually died in 1893. Supported by his uncle, Arthur was sent to the Roman Catholic Jesuit preparatory school Hodder Place, Stonyhurst, in 1868 when he was eight. After this, he attended Stonyhurst College from where he received his graduation degree in 1875. Between 1876 and 1881, Arthur studied medicine at the University of Edinburgh and started writing short stories. He received his doctorate with specialization in *tabes dorsalis* in 1885.

In 1890, Arthur settled in London and began practising as an ophthalmologist. The practice was not successful and again he turned to writing more and more. Arthur, as a writer, was always inclined towards writing historical novels and believed that the success of Sherlock Holmes came as a hurdle in this. He decided to kill the character of Sherlock Holmes and did so in the story *The Final Problem* in 1893. A public hullabaloo ensued and he had to bring the character back in the story *The Adventures of the Empty House.*

In his later career, Arthur moved on to a broader line of work and began writing about the political sphere. One of such was *The War in South Africa: Its Cause and Conduct,* a pamphlet which explained the involvement of UK in the Boer War. He next wrote *The Great Boer War* in 1900. The success of the pamphlet led him to being elected for Knighthood in 1902 and he was made Deputy-Lieutenant of Surrey. *The Crime of the Congo,* another pamphlet was published in 1909, after which he wrote what is believed to be one of his masterpieces *The Lost World* in 1912.

In the early 20th century, Arthur suffered from many personal losses. His wife Louisa died of tuberculosis and tragedy once again hit the family when his son Kingsley, brother Innes, and other close relatives succumbed to death one after another. These incidents pushed him into a state of depression and turned him into a spiritualist. Arthur, as a child, was an agonist and had strayed from religious nature for many years. However, by this time he had become increasingly interested and obsessed with spiritualism to the extent that he wrote a novel called *The Land of Mist.* His next book *The Coming of the Fairies,* which he wrote in 1921, supported his views on spiritualism and "life beyond life". In his book *The History of Spiritualism,* Arthur endorsed the spirit materialization and psychic phenomena. By this time he had come to believe that the living can communicate with the dead. *The Case Book of Sherlock Holmes,* one of his last books, was published in 1927.

Arthur Conan Doyle died of heart attack in the family garden in Windlesham, Crowborough, on 7 July, 1930 and was buried in the Church Yard at Minstead in New Forest, Hampshire, in England. His wife Jean was buried at his side after her death in 1940.

RABINDRANATH TAGORE

(07.05.1861 – 07.08.1941)

Rabindranath Tagore was born on May 7, 1861 in a wealthy Brahmin family in Calcutta, now Kolkata. He was the ninth son of Debendranath and Sarada Devi. His grandfather Dwarkanath Tagore was a rich landlord and social reformer. Rabindranath Tagore had his initial education in Oriental Seminary School. But he did not like the conventional education and started studying at home under several teachers. After undergoing his *upanayan* (coming-of-age) rite at the age of eleven, Tagore and his father left Calcutta in 1873 to tour India for several months, visiting his father's Santiniketan estate and Amritsar before reaching the Himalayan hill station of Dalhousie. There, Tagore read biographies, studied history, astronomy, modern science, and Sanskrit, and examined the classical poetry of Kalidasa.

In 1874, Tagore's poem 'Abhilaasha' (Desire) was published anonymously in a magazine called *Tattobodhini.* Tagore's mother Sarada Devi expired in 1875. Rabindranath's first book of poems, *Kabi Kahini* (Tale of a Poet) was published in 1878. In the same year Tagore sailed to England with his elder brother Satyendranath to study law. But he returned to India in 1880 and started his career as a poet and writer. In 1883, Rabindranath Tagore married Mrinalini Devi Raichaudhuri, with whom he had two sons and three daughters.

In 1884, Tagore wrote a collection of poems *Kori-o-Kamal* (Sharp and Flats). He also wrote dramas – *Raja-o-Rani* (King and Queen) and *Visarjan* (Sacrifice). In 1890, Rabindranath Tagore moved to Shilaidaha (now in Bangladesh) to look after the family estate. Between 1893 and 1900 Tagore wrote seven volumes of poetry, which included *Sonar Tari* (The Golden Boat) and *Khanika.* In 1901, Rabindranath Tagore became the editor of the magazine *Bangadarshan.* He established Bolpur Brahmachari Ashram at Shantiniketan, a school based on the pattern of old Indian ashramas. In 1902, his wife Mrinalini died. Tagore composed *Smaran* (In Memoriam), a collection of poems, dedicated to his wife.

In 1905, Lord Curzon decided to divide Bengal into two parts. Rabindranath Tagore strongly protested against this decision. Tagore wrote a number of national songs and attended protest meetings. He introduced the Rakhibandhan ceremony, symbolising the underlying unity of undivided Bengal.

In 1909, Rabindranath Tagore started writing *Gitanjali.* In 1912, he went to Europe for the second time. On the journey to London he translated some of his poems/songs from *Gitanjali* into English. He met William Rothenstein, a noted British painter, in London. Rothenstein was impressed by the poems, made copies and gave them to Yeats and other English poets. Yeats was enthralled. He later wrote the introduction to *Gitanjali* when it was published in September 1912 in a limited edition by the India Society in London. Rabindranath Tagore was awarded Nobel Prize for Literature in 1913 for *Gitanjali.* In 1915 he was knighted by the British King George V.

In 1919, following the Jallianwala Bagh massacre, Tagore renounced his knighthood. He was a supporter of Gandhiji but stayed out of politics. He was opposed to nationalism and militarism as a matter of principle, and instead promoted spiritual values and the creation of a new world culture founded in multi-culturalism, diversity and tolerance. Unable to gain ideological support to his views, he retired into relative solitude. Between the years 1916 and 1934 he travelled widely.

1n 1921, Rabindranath Tagore established Viswabharati University. He gave all his money from Nobel Prize and royalty money from his books to this University. Tagore was not only a creative genius, he was quite knowledgeable in Western culture, especially Western poetry and science, too. Tagore had a good grasp of modern – post-Newtonian – physics, and was well able to hold his own in a debate with Einstein in 1930 on the newly emerging principles of quantum mechanics and chaos. His meetings and tape recorded conversations with his contemporaries such as Albert Einstein and H.G. Wells, epitomize his brilliance.

In 1940 Oxford University arranged a special ceremony in Santiniketan and awarded Rabindranath Tagore with Doctorate of Literature. Gurudev Rabindranath Tagore passed away on August 7, 1941 in his ancestral home in Calcutta.

Rabindranath Tagore was the first Asian to become a Nobel laureate when he won The Nobel Prize for his collection of poems, *Gitanjali,* in 1913; was awarded knighthood by the British King George V; and established The Viswabharati University.

Rabindranath Tagore was an icon of Indian culture. He was a poet, philosopher, musician, writer, and educationist. He was popularly called as 'Gurudev' and his songs were popularly known as Rabindra Sangeet. Two songs from his canon are now the national anthems of India and Bangladesh: the Jana Gana Mana and the Amar Shonar Bangla.

RUDYARD KIPLING

(30.12.1865 – 18.01.1936)

Joseph Rudyard Kipling was an English author, journalist and poet who wrote the famous fiction *The Jungle Book.* Born in the British India, Bombay, he worked in India with a much renowned newspaper, *The Pioneer,* Allahabad, before taking up writing as a profession. Best known for his works such as *The Jungle Book, Kim* and *Just So Stories for Little Children,* Kipling ranks among the greatest English novelists and authors and is regarded as the leader of the art of the short stories. The author has written a number of stories including the famous, *The Man Who Would Be King,* and several poems and short stories and contributed greatly to English literature during the 19th and 20th century. The author received the honorary Nobel Peace Prize in Literature in 1907 and became the first English writer and the youngest recipient to have received the award till this day.

Joseph Rudyard Kipling was born on 30 December, 1865 in Bombay, British India. His father Lockwood Kipling was a sculptor and the head of department of the architectural sculpture at the Sir Jamsetjee Jeejeebhoy School of Art and Industry in Bombay. Rudyard's mother Alice Kipling was a lively and cheerful woman. After spending some fabulous years in India, a six year old Kipling was sent to England where they lived with a couple Mr. and Mrs. Holloway as then was the custom for the British nationalists living in India. He was accompanied by his three year old sister Alice.

Those years under the bullying and maltreatment of Mrs. Holloway, were of humiliation, torture and obloquy as he sardonically recalls in his autobiography. However, they received the due love and affection at their maternal aunt Georgia's home that was denied at Holloway's. The bad days came to an end in 1877, when Alice Kipling returned to England and took them away with her. The next year in 1878, Rudyard was sent to study at the United Service College at Westward Ho in Devon. Due to the financial difficulties of his parents, Rudyard abandoned his dream to study at Oxford and took up a job in Lahore - then a part of India - of an assistant editor in a local newspaper the *Civil & Military Gazette.*

While in Lahore, Kipling wrote over thirty stories for *The Gazette* beginning from the year 1886. In 1888, his first prose collection *Plain Tales from the Hills* was published in Calcutta. In 1887, Kipling became a part of a much renowned newspaper *The Pioneer,* Allahabad. Whilst working with the paper, Rudyard kept on writing and published six volumes of short stories including *In Black and White, Soldiers Three* and *The Phantom Rickshaw.* In 1889, he left the newspaper in response to a fall out with the authorities. He decided to move on to London to make his entry in the literary world there. He left India on 8 March 1889.

Several significant things happened in the next two years of his life: he wrote his first novel, *The Light That Failed* in 1891, and also met an American author and publishing agent, Wolcott Ballisterwith with whom he worked together on a novel, *The Naulakha.* In the meantime, he also suffered from a nervous breakdown. Due to his continuously deteriorating health, his doctors advised him for a sea voyage, which he eventually embarked on in 1891 with the intention of visiting

South Africa, Australia, New Zealand and India once again. However, his plans were cut short on account of the sudden demise of Wolcott Balestier from typhoid fever, and he immediately decided to return to London. Meanwhile, he wrote a collection of short stories about British India called *Life's Handicap* which was published in 1891 in London.

In 1902, Kipling published another story *Just So Stories for Little Children* which would become one of his most acclaimed works following the success of *Kim.* He further wrote two science fiction *With the Night Mail* and *As Easy as A.B.C.* which made into print in 1905 and 1912 respectively.

The most active phase of his life was the first decade of 20th century, when he was at the peak of his creative best. For him, 1907 brought along with it the greatest honour of the time, the Noble Prize for Literature. At the award function in Stockholm on 10 December 1907, Kipling became the first English language recipient of this great honour.

After this great accomplishment, came two great poetry and story compendiums: *Puck of Pook's Hill* and *Reward and Fairies* which were published in 1906 and 1910 respectively. The latter contained one of the most favourite poems of all times in English literature called "If..." This marvellous poem inciting readers for self-command and phlegm became Kipling's one of the most famous poetry creation of all the times.

Kipling always remained politically expressive with his creations. He commiserated with the Anti-Home Rule stand of the Irish Unionist Party. He also stroked chords of intellectuality with the Dublin-born leader Edward Carson who raised a potent voice against "Home Rule" and also publicised his staunch opinion through his creations. Kipling also projected himself as a strong opponent of the Principles of Democratic Centralism and Quasi-military Discipline through his creations.

Despite his intellectual assets and enormous popularity, he was never made Poet Laureate. Different people quote different reasons behind it, some are of the view that he himself turned down the offer while others are of the opinion that Queen Victoria didn't approve of him. However, this never came as a hurdle in Kipling's literary career, he is still regarded as the best author and poet English Language could ever get.

Tragedy once again hit the family when his only son John Kipling died in 1915 at the 'Battle of Loos'. The untimely death of his son made Rudyard blame himself for his role in getting John in the Army at an early age of 17. The incident made him write a poem "My Boy Jack" in which he deeply mourns for his son cursing and blaming himself.

In the year 1922, Kipling was elected the Lord Rector of St Andrews University in Scotland and remained on the position till 1925. Towards the end of his life, Kipling chose to take a backseat with his writing career, though he did not completely abandon it, the output was lesser. He died of a haemorrhage on 18 January, 1936 and was cremated at Golden Green Crematorium.

SRI AUROBINDO

(15.08.1872 – 05.12.1950)

Sri Aurobindo was born on 15th August, 1872, to an anglicised father Dr Krishnadhan Ghosh. He wanted his children to be schooled in English, therefore at the age of 7 Aurobindo was sent to study in England. Aurobindo studied first at St Paul's, London, and then at King's College, Cambridge. Life in England was often tough for Aurobindo; resources were meagre and for many years he had to often survive on a frugal diet. However, he proved to be a scholar of great intellect and capacity. He mastered the classics and English poetry (later he wrote extensively on the English poets). The famous don Oscar Browning declared Aurobindo one of the greatest scholars he had seen.

It was at Cambridge University that Aurobindo first became aware of the plight of his country, at the time under the rule of the British. Aurobindo became inspired to join a society committed to overthrowing the British rule. This period was an important landmark in Aurobindo's life. With his new political perspective he turned down an opportunity to join the British Civil Service. He had passed all his exams but failed to turn up for the obligatory horse riding test. Therefore at the age of 21 he returned to India increasingly committed to working for Indian independence.

On his return to Indian soil Aurobindo was overwhelmed with a feeling of intense inner peace. This experience came unsought and was an indication of his future spiritual capacity. However, at the time Aurobindo's main concern and main passion was political independence of his beloved motherland. Aurobindo threw himself into revolutionary politics, associating with the great figures of Bengal such as Bipin Chandra Pal and B.C. Chatterji. He was dismayed with the weakness of Congress and argued for direct action aiming for complete independence. Through his journal *Bande Mataram,* Aurobindo was the first leader to call for the full independence for India.

For several years Aurobindo was a pivotal figure in the movement for independence. He had the qualities of a natural leader but was always happy to work in the background as much as possible. It was during this period that Aurobindo also became increasingly interested in Yoga and meditation. Whilst engaged in spiritual disciplines Aurobindo came across a teacher of meditation, Lele Maharaj. He taught Aurobindo how to control thoughts and not let them enter into his mind. Aurobindo followed his instructions to the letter and within three days he succeeded in completely emptying the mind and entered into a state of nirvana. This same experience had taken Lele Maharaj over six years to attain. Lele Maharaj was amazed at the progress of the young Aurobindo.

However, it was the political struggle which held the greatest sway on Aurobindo, the freedom of India was his primary concern. After a fatal incident involving revolutionaries, Aurobindo became a marked man. In 1908 he was arrested for the possession of weapons and was held in jail for a year before his case came to court. His trial became a major event with much attention placed on the incident. The evidence against Aurobindo was quite weighty and he feared he would be convicted. However, Aurobindo was fortunate to have C.R. Das as his defence lawyer. C.R. Das threw himself heart and soul into Aurobindo's defence.

His commitment and capacity meant that Aurobindo felt completely assured and did not have to even concern himself with his own defence.

It was during this time that he became conscious about his inner self. He practised meditation in his cell, read about the ancient principles of yoga and realized the omnipresence of God. Becoming aware of a divine inner guidance, Aurobindo listened to his inner command, which instructed him to leave politics and work for the renewal of Sanatana Dharma, 'the eternal religion'. After coming out of the jail, he came in contact with Sister Nivedita, a disciple of Swami Vivekananda. Thereafter, he changed his abode from Calcutta to Pondicherry and devoted himself completely spiritual disciplines. Aurobindo also became a prolific writer, producing many articles, writings and poetry. Eventually, Pondicherry became a mecca for spiritual seekers.

Founded on November 24, 1926, Sri Aurobindo Ashram had only 24 disciples in its early days. In the month of December, the same year, a French woman, Mirra Alfassa, arrived in the ashram. Determined to withdraw from public view, Sri Aurobindo entrusted her with the working of the ashram. Mirra was popularly called Mother, and with time, in the ashram came to be known as 'The Mother'. The ashram that started as a small organization grew into a dynamic spiritual community and is operational even in the present times. It has branches in cities all over the world, apart from the downtown area of Pondicherry.

Though Sri Aurobindo retreated from his ashram life in November 1926, he spent hours replying to the letters of his disciples and followers. His letters gave him the opportunity to explain about yoga and its applications. Sri Aurobindo brought relief and respite to his followers and released them from their pain, fear and anxiety. Apart from his spiritual mission, he also took interest in the political scenario of the world.

Sri Aurobindo believed that every religion was right in its own way. A poet, philosopher, writer and spiritual master, he offered a new vision of yoga and a spiritual path that could be followed by his disciples. Out of his many works, one of the most praiseworthy is The Life Divine, a comprehensive explanation of his Integral Yoga. Sri Aurobindo died on 5th December, 1950, refusing to undergo any surgery or even healing himself on his own. He believed that by leaving for the heavenly abode, he would effectively continue his spiritual mission.

SOMERSET MAUGHAM

(25.01.1874–16.12.1965)

William Somerset Maugham was a famous English author, novelist and playwright. His popularity lies in the fact that by early 1930s, he had become the highest paid author of his era. His most famous works include novels *Of Human Bondage, The Razor's Edge* and *The Moon and Sixpence* and short stories *Footprints In The Jungle, Rain* and *The Outstation. Of Human Bondage* – a semi autographical book – is a reflection of his own childhood. The main character of the book Philip earned international attention who was orphaned and raised by his pious uncle like Maugham. During the peak of his popularity, Maugham also earned praise as one of the most significant travel writers. *The Gentleman in the Parlour,* an account of his travels to Burma, Vietnam and Cambodia, is considered his best work in this genre. Many of his short stories and novels have been adapted for radio and television.

Maugham was born on 25 January, 1874 in Paris in an English family. His father was an English lawyer and solicitor to the British Embassy in Paris. His grandfather was also an English lawyer and a cofounder of the English Law Society and it was expected that Maugham would follow his father and grandfather in their successful legal career. His brother Viscount Maugham followed the elders in their footsteps and became a Lord Chancellor. However, Maugham did not show any willingness towards their legacy.

Maugham's mother Edith Mary died at the age of 41, followed by his father two years later. Now orphaned,

Maugham was moved to England to his uncle's place. His uncle Henry Maugham, the Vicar of Whistable, proved to be cold and emotionally cruel to the young Maugham and his unsympathetic treatment would lead him to develop a stammer. Maugham was sent to the King's Canterbury which proved to be the extension of the humiliation and indifference he suffered at home.

Life became miserable and he left the school at the age of sixteen. He moved to Germany where he enrolled in Heidelberg University to study literature, philosophy and German. During his stay in Germany, Maugham first acknowledged his homosexuality after his first sexual encounter with John Ellingham Brooks. On the completion of his degree there, Maugham returned to England and found a position in an accountant's office with his uncle's help. Though he left the job soon and it further displeased his uncle, he finally persuaded him into the profession of medicine and sent him to the King's College, London, where he spent another five years studying medicine.

By the late 1914, Maugham had become famous and had published as many as ten plays and ten novels. With the onset of the World War I, he joined the British Red Cross' Literary Ambulance Drivers, with other 23 popular writers including E. E. Cummings and Ernest Hemingway. He continued to produce novels and edit previous works. *Of Human Bondage,* another novel written during this period and his masterpiece, appeared in 1905 and received a mixed reaction initially from the literary society of England. However, it gained popularity with time and it has since never been out of print.

In 1916, Maugham embarked upon writing *The Moon and Sixpence,* a novel based upon the life of Paul Gauguin.

He voyaged to the Pacific for the necessary research work accompanied by Haxton, his companion and a long time lover. During this period he wrote *Ashenden,* a collection of short stories about a gentleman and indifferent spy. In 1922, Maugham produced a book of 58 short story sketches, based upon his travels to China and Hong Kong. Maugham's play *The Letter,* was performed in London in 1927 and was later adapted into a film in 1929 and then in 1940. With the collapse of France, he left the country, though his prodigious output of play and novels continued to emerge and he became the most popular and highest paid writer in English literature.

Among his most important works is the novel *Of Human Bondage* and is also considered his masterpiece. The novel is a semi–autobiography with the main character Philip Carey depicted as an orphaned child, like Maugham, and brought up by his self-righteous uncle. Another novel *The Moon and Sixpence,* which gave him stunning success, is a real life-based story of Paul Gauguin. One of his most famous novels, *The Razor's Edge* was published in 1944 and has been adapted in to movies.

SAROJINI NAIDU

(13.02.1879 – 02.03.1949)

Sarojini Chattopadhyay was born at Hyderabad on February 13, 1879, the eldest of a large family, all of whom were taught English at an early age. At the age of twelve she passed the matriculation of the Madras University, and awoke to find herself famous throughout India.

Sarojini was a bright child who passed her matriculation at the age of 12 standing first in the Madras Presidency. She studied at the King's College, London, and Girton College, Cambridge, for a while. During this period her creative urge found expression in poems. She also happened to be a good singer. Her ability to sing charmingly fetched her the title 'Nightingale of India'. After 1917 she stepped into active politics. In 1898 she married Dr. Govindarajulu Naidu.

Before she was fifteen the great struggle of her life began. Dr. Govindarajulu Naidu, later to become her husband, was, though of an old and honourable family, not a Brahmin. The difference of caste roused an equal opposition, not only on the side of her family, but of his; and in 1895 she was sent to England, against her will, with a special scholarship from the Nizam. She remained in England, with an interval of travel in Italy, till 1898, studying first at King's College, London, then, till her health again broke down, at Girton. She returned to Hyderabad in September 1898, and in the December of that year, to the scandal of all India, broke through the bonds of caste and married Dr. Naidu.

Educated in Hyderabad and later in Madras, she excelled in her studies and earned fame all over India. At sixteen, she earned a scholarship and was sent to London and Cambridge for further studies but failed to gain the same level of academic success (partially due to illness as well as restlessness, as she readily admits) and came back to India. While Sarojini's poetic sensibilities began early - she wrote a prodigious one thousand three-hundred line poem at the age of thirteen - it was during her studies in England where she began writing her poems that later comprised the bulk of her first significant collection, the best-selling *The Golden Threshold.* Subsequent years were spent quietly by the young Sarojini, content by raising her four children and tending to her domestic work.

During her stay in England she met Arthur Symons, a poet and critic. They corresponded after her return to India. After that, she published two other collections of poems– *The Bird of Time* and *The Broken Wings*. In 1918, *Feast of Youth* was published. Later, *The Magic Tree, The Wizard Mask* and *A Treasury of Poems* were published. Maharshi Arvind, Rabindranath Tagore and Jawaharlal Nehru were among the thousands of admirers of her work. Her poems had English words, but an Indian soul.

Then in 1916, she met Mahatma Gandhi, and she totally directed her energy to the fight for India's freedom. She would roam around the country like a general of the army and pour enthusiasm among the hearts of Indians. The independence of India became the heart and soul of her work.

She was responsible for awakening the women of India. She brought them out of the kitchen. She travelled from state to state, city after city and asked for the rights of the women. She re-established self-esteem in the women of India.

In 1925, she chaired the summit of Congress in Kanpur. In 1928, she went to the USA with the message of the non-violence movement from Gandhiji. When in 1930, Gandhiji was arrested for a protest, she took the helms of his movement. In 1931, she participated in the Round Table Summit, along with Gandhiji and Pundit Malaviyaji. In 1942, she was arrested during the "Quit India" protest and stayed in jail for 21 months with Gandhiji.

After independence she became the Governor of Uttar Pradesh. She was the first woman governor. She passed away on March 2, 1949.

PREMCHAND

(31.07.1880 – 08.10.1936)

An extremely famous name that comes to mind when we talk of Urdu novel writers is that of Munshi Premchand. The life history of Premchand is like that of any ordinary man. But what makes him stand out are the numerous works he composed in his lifetime. They are still read with much enthusiasm and admiration. Though he had financial crunches all through his life, he had the rich collection of his works and compositions.

Premchand was popularly known as Munshi Premchand and was one of the greatest literary figures of modern Hindi literature. His stories vividly portrayed the social scenario of those times.

Premchand's real name was Dhanpat Rai Srivastava. He was born on July 31, 1880 in Lamahi near Varanasi where his father Munshi Ajayab Lal was a clerk in the post office. Premchand lost his mother when he was just seven years old. His father married again. Premchand was very close to his elder sister. His early education was in a madarsa under a Maulavi, where he learnt Urdu. When he was studying in the ninth class he was married, much against his wishes. He was only fifteen years old at that time.

Premchand lost his father when he was sixteen years old. Premchand was left responsible for his stepmother and stepsiblings. He earned five rupees a month tutoring a lawyer's child. Premchand passed his matriculation exam with great effort and took up a teaching position, with a monthly salary of eighteen rupees. While working, he studied privately and passed his Intermediate and B. A. examinations. Later, Premchand worked as the deputy sub-inspector of schools in what was then the United Provinces.

In 1910, he was hauled up by the District Magistrate in Jamirpur for his anthology of short stories *Soz-e-Watan* (Dirge of the Nation), which was labelled seditious. His book *Soz-e-Watan* was banned by the then British government, which burnt all of the copies. Initially Premchand wrote in Urdu under the name of Nawab Rai. However, when his novel *Soz-e-Watan* was confiscated by the British, he started writing under the pseudonym Premchand.

Before Premchand, Hindi literature consisted mainly of fantasy or religious works. Premchand brought realism to Hindi literature. He wrote over 300 stories, a dozen novels and two plays. The stories have been compiled and published as *Mansarovar.* His famous creations are: *Panch Parameshvar, Idgah, Shatranj Ke Khiladi, Poos Ki Raat, Bade Ghar Ki Beti, Kafan, Udhar Ki Ghadi, Namak Ka Daroga, Gaban, Godaan,* and *Nirmala.*

Premchand was a great social reformer; he married a child widow named Shivarani Devi. She wrote a book on him, *Premchand Ghar Mein* after his death. In 1921 he answered Gandhiji's call and resigned from his job. He worked to generate patriotism and nationalistic sentiments in the general populace. When the editor of the journal *Maryada* was jailed in the freedom movement, Premchand worked for a time as the editor of that journal. Afterwards, he worked as the principal in a school of Kashi Vidyapeeth.

The main characteristics of Premchand's writings is his interesting storytelling and use of simple language. His novels describe the problems of rural and urban India. He avoided the use of highly Sanskritized Hindi and instead used the dialect of the common people. Premchand wrote on the realistic issues of the day - communalism, corruption, zamindari, debt, poverty, colonialism etc.

Premchand brought realism to Hindi literature. His writings have been translated not only into all Indian languages, but also Russian, Chinese, and many other foreign languages. He died in October 8, 1936.

VIRGINIA WOOLF

(25.01.1882–28.03.1941)

Virginia Woolf was an English writer, author and novelist and a pioneer of modernism in English literature. Among her most famous work are novels *To the Lighthouse, Mrs. Dalloway* and *Orlando* and an essay *A Room of One's Own.* She was an important figure in the Victorian literary society and is regarded as one of the greatest modernist literary personality of the twentieth century. She became the innovator of the English literature with her experiment with the 'stream of consciousness' and broke the mold with her highly experimental language denouncing the traditional literary techniques. Her works allow for a deeper insight into the psychology of a character and its real thinking, though they are often criticised for its pretentious and elitist depiction of the characters. The author turned into a victim to a severe depression cluttering her life and mental stability and eventually leading her to commit suicide in 1941.

Virginia Woolf, originally Adeline Virginia Stephen, was born on 25 January, 1882 to her father Sir Leslie Stephen, a renowned author, and mother Julia Prinsep Stephen. Julia Stephen was born in India who later on moved to England permanently, whereupon she worked as a model for painters and photographers. Both Leslie and Julia had been married previously and been widowed and had children from their marriage staying with them. The couple had four children with their own marriage. Thus the young Virginia grew up with a number of half brothers and sisters around her.

As a result of her parents' connection to the eminent writers such as William Thackeray and George Henry Lewes, Virginia was raised in an environment influenced with Victorian literary society. Her own father was a noble writer, editor and critic who was married to the eldest daughter of William Thackeray. Virginia developed an early liking for the English literature and as a result, was trained in the classics and English literature, whereas her brothers received only formal education.

Most of her initial years were spent in Cornwall where she first became interested in natural beauty. The impression of its landscapes and the lighthouse imprinted on her mind and would come out in her literary works. Except for the initial few years, Virginia did not have a very happy childhood. Her mother passed away in 1895 followed by her sister who died two years later. She was shattered at the very first acquaintance with the reality of inevitable death and before she could get over the initial shock, her father died in 1904. She lost her mental stability and suffered from her first nervous breakdown during this period.

She was briefly institutionalised when these bouts of depression continued to occur. According to her biographer and close relative Quentin Bell, these depressive breakdowns were also a result of the sexual abuse she was subjected to by her half brothers George and Gerald. Virginia's memoir *A Sketch of the Past* reveals these facts, which she wrote much later in her life. The mental illness cause during this period would plague her throughout her life and have a drastic effect on her social life, eventually causing her to suicide, though it hardly affected her literary talents.

In 1917, they two founded the Hogarth Press and wrote a few books in collaboration. Her most popular works during this period include *Night and Day* (1919), a short story collection *Monday or Tuesday* (1921) and essays in *The Common Reader* (1925). *Jacob's Room* (1922) and *Mrs. Dalloway* (1925) which was adapted into the film *The Hours* in 2002, *To the Lighthouse* (1927) and *Orlando: A Biography* (1928).

Virginia's first professional writing began in 1905, when she started writing for the *Times Literary Supplement.* However, her first individual work, a novel *The Voyage Out* was published in 1915. The book was published by her half brother's imprint Gerald Duckworth and Company Limited. The content of the book was later modified by Louise DeSalvo. Most of her works were published by her own Hogarth Press.

By this time, Woolf had become a famous personality in the Victorian literary society and was often regarded as the greatest novelist of the twentieth century and a forerunner of modernism. She became an innovator of the English literature with her successful experiment with the 'stream of consciousness' psychological and emotional motives of the characters. Her novels are marked with narrative style, passionate lyricism and stylistic intelligence.

To the Lighthouse, a semi-autobiographical piece published in 1921, depicts the Ramsay family's visit to a lighthouse. The novel also portrays the lives of a nation's natives trapped in a war. Another famous novel *The Waves,* displays a group of friends who construct the plot of the novel. *Between the Acts,* her last piece of work, which was published in 1941, reflects her experience with art, sexual ambivalence and life in a symbolic and narrative style. Most of the works have been translated into a number of foreign languages and have been adapted into films and cinema.

Woolf's eminence came to a downfall with the end of the World War II which was again restored with the Feminist criticism around 1970s. She was also criticised for her anti-semitism and snobbery, which she herself had admitted in her personal diary. Her literary efforts were often targeted for what they feel "exemplifying the English upper-middle intellectual class".

Virginia Woolf was writing what was to be her last publication, *Between the Acts,* published in 1941. The monstrous bouts of depression had come back and once again she began to experience fear and fright. The outbreak of World War II and the destruction of her London house exacerbated her condition until she could not write a single paragraph properly. She was well aware of her illness, as her letters show, and decided to spare her husband the pain and trouble caused by her frequent bouts of illness.

On 28 March 1941, Woolf committed suicide by drowning herself into the River Ouse, filling her coat's pockets with stones. Her body was found on 18 April, and was buried by her husband in the garden of their house in Sussex. Leonard set to the task of completing her unfinished works and editing her prodigious collection of journals. He died in 1960. Virginia Woolf's posthumously published works include *The Death of the Moth and Other Essays* (1942), *A Haunted House and Other Short Stories* (1944), and *The Moment and Other Essays* (1948). An award-winning biography of Woolf was written by her nephew Professor Quentin Bell, entitled as *Virginia Woolf: A Biography.*

KHALIL GIBRAN

(06.01.1883 – 1923)

Khalil Gibran was a Lebanese American artist, writer, philosopher and the third most popular poet in history after Shakespeare and Laotse. Born in an underprivileged and deprived family, Khalil rose to the level of world renowned author and artist despite the adverse circumstances he often landed into. As an artist, he has also created some of the most fascinating drawings during his lifetime. His bestselling book *The Prophet,* a collection of 26 splendid poems, has been translated into over 20 foreign languages.

Gibran was born on 6 January, 1883 in a Christian town of modern day Lebanon. His mother Kamila, who was from a Christian family had married twice before marrying his father whose name was also Khalil and had a son Peter from her previous marriage. Later, the young Khalil's two siblings, both girls, Mariana and Sultana were born. His father Khalil, however, proved to be an irresponsible father and husband and became so indebted from gambling that the family lost almost all its property.

Due to family's abject poverty, young Gibran was deprived of the formal schooling though he was often visited by priests who taught him about Bible and other languages. The conditions worsened when his father, who was a tax collector, was arrested for alleged fraud. When he was released by the authorities in 1894, the family had lost its last asset; their home. It was then, that his mother Kamila decided to move to the United States along with her children to make a life far from her husband. The family left for New York on 25 June 1895.

In the United States, Gibran's family stayed in Boston's South End, which was the second largest Lebanese-American community at that time. His mother began to work as a peddler selling things door to door and the family suffered from many other hardships there until Peter was grown enough to take up the major responsibilities of the family. Meanwhile, Khalil was sent to a school especially for immigrants in 1895 and later to an art school in the same year where he caught his teacher's eye with his promising drawings.

In 1898, Gibran returned to Lebanon where he studied at a preparatory school and later enrolled into a higher studies institute in Beirut. In 1902, his younger sister Sultana died of tuberculosis before he could return to them in the United States. His brother Peter died of the same disease the following year. Already shattered by the death of his siblings, Khalil lost his mother in the same year who died of cancer. It was his younger sister Mariana, who consoled and supported him during this toughest time of his life.

Khalil devoted himself to his childhood passion for drawings and organized his first exhibition in 1904, where he met Mary Elizabeth Haskell who was a headmistress and ten years senior to him. The relationship between them which started with a casual friendship became more intimate as time passed and had a great influence in Khalil's later life. In 1908, Gibran enrolled into an Arts College in Paris and studied there for two years before going to Boston. As a native of Lebanon, Khalil's works were extensively in Arabic and other Syrian languages, before he acquired proficiency in the English language and most of his works published after 1918, were in English. His first book was *The Madman,* which was published in 1918. While in New York, he became associated with the New York Pen League, an organization formed by Lebanese-American immigrant poets.

Gibran's early works were largely influenced with Christianity and he wrote several books based upon Christian beliefs and sometimes contradicting it. One of such work was *Jesus, The Son of Man.* His bestselling book, *The Prophet,* which is a masterpiece of 26 poetic essays, became a landslide success and remains so till this day. The book was first published in 1923, and since then it has been translated into over 20 languages. It was ranked as the most popular book of the 20th century in America. His other notable work was *Sand and Foam* that became famous for its quotes.

A Syrian nationalist, Gibran wrote a political draft in 1911, where he showed his unwavering allegiance and commitment to his country and its territorial integrity. Despite being a great supporter of internationalism, he believed in Syrian nationalism, which was distinguished from Lebanese or Arab nationalism. Furthermore, he also demanded for the adoption of Arabic as a national language of Syria.

SINCLAIR LEWIS

(07.02.1885 – 10.01.1951)

Harry Sinclair Lewis was born in Sauk Centre, a prairie village in the heart of Minnesota, as the third son of a country doctor. His mother, who was the daughter of a Canadian physician, died of tuberculosis when Lewis was six years old. His father remarried a year later Isabel Warner. Lewis considered her psychically his own mother. Later Lewis characterised Sauk Centre "narrow-minded and socially provincial" and books offered him one way of escape: he had access to the three or four hundred volumes, exclusive of medical books, in his father's library.

Lewis's early life was made miserable by teasing – he was strange-looking with his red hair and very bad skin. At the age of 13 he ran away from home to become a drummer boy in the Spanish-American War, but his father caught up with him at the railroad station, and brought the boy home. Lewis started to write and keep a diary in his youth; he produced romantic poetry, and stories about knights and fair ladies. Before 1921 he had already published six novels.

In 1902 Lewis entered the Oberlin Academy, but then moved to Yale University and started to contribute to the *Yale Literary Magazine*. On one summer vacation Lewis travelled to England on a cattle boat and in another year, dissatisfied with college, he went to Panama in search of a job on the canal. He also worked as a janitor at Upton Sinclair's socialist commune Helicon Hall (1906-07). For a period he tried to earn his living as a free-lance writer in

New York. In Yale Lewis met Jack London, and later he sold the elder writer short story plots.

Lewis received his M.A. in 1908 and worked for publishing houses and various magazines in Iowa, Carmel, San Francisco, Washington D.C. and New York City. In Greenwich Village he associated occasionally with such radicals as John Reed and Floyd Dell. For a short time he was a member of the Socialist Party. Lewis's first published book was *Hike and the Aeroplane* (1912), which appeared under the pseudonym Tom Graham. The next work, *Our Mr Wrenn* (1914) presented a hero, who is innocent, naïve, and who dreams of adventures. After travels abroad he returns to his normal idyllic life. Similar characters populate Lewis's further novels, among them Carol Kennicott from the novel *Main Street* (1920).

From 1913-14 Lewis produced a syndicated book page, which helped him to gain good reviews of his own works by his fellow writers. In 1914 Lewis married Grace Livingston Hegger, an editor at *Vogue.* Their son, Wells, was named after the famous British author H.G. Wells, to whose social ideas Lewis was drawn. For the following two years he worked as an editor and advertising manager at the book publishing firm George H. Doran Company. In 1916 Lewis abandoned his job and travelled with his wife around the country.

After publishing two novels, Lewis devoted himself entirely to writing. He gained fame with *Main Street,* a study of idealism and reality in a narrow-minded small-town. "*Main Street* is the continuation of Main Streets everywhere." It meant cheap shops, ugly public buildings, and citizens who were bound by rigid conventions. The protagonist, Carol Kennicott, is an emancipated woman, who is in conflict with the conformity of Gopher Prairie –

gopher is a large rodent living in the western states of the U.S. Before marrying Dr Will Kennicott of Gopher Prairie, Carol has studied library science in Chicago and worked in St. Paul, Minnesota. The town is far from the romantic picture of open and democratic American community. Carol joins the clubs, the Library Board to encourage reading, and learns to play bridge, but she soon finds out that unions and profit-sharing are dangerous subjects in conversation. After flirting with a lawyer, she meets a young Swedish sailor, who leaves the town, before they start to do something else than talk and walk together. She leaves her family, and moves to Washington, DC. Erik finds his way to Hollywood, and Carol returns to Gopher Prairie, but without feeling defeated: "I do not admit that Main Street is as beautiful as it should be! I do not admit that dish-washing is enough to satisfy all women!" The book had parallels with the author's own early life. Carol also has skin problems. Lewis claimed that Main Street was read "with the same masochistic pleasure that one has in sucking an aching tooth."

John Ford's film version of *Arrowsmith* from 1931 was produced by Samuel Goldwyn. Ford was faithful to the novel's themes, but he made the Midwestern doctor more pompous than Lewis intended. At Goldwyn's request, Ford promised not to drink during the shooting of the film. However, the director walked off the picture after some troubles and boozed on Catalina Island. Finally, he was removed by Goldwyn.

SUKUMAR ROY

(1887 – 1923)

Sukumar Roy, children's writer, was born in Calcutta (now, Kolkata) on 30 October, 1887. His family was originally from Masua in Mymensingh. His father, Upendra Kishore Roychowdhury, who also wrote for children, was a musician and mechanic and his son was the Oscar-winning filmmaker Satyajit Roy.

After passing the Entrance examination from the City School, Sukumar Roy took his B.Sc. (1911) in chemistry from Presidency College. He then went to England on the Guruprasanna Ghosh Scholarship to study photography and printing technology. Sukumar studied at the Manchester School of Technology, where he proved the effectiveness of photo printing in halftone invented by his father.

At the East and West Society, Sukumar Roy read an essay called 'Spirit of Rabindranath', which was later published in the *Quest* magazine. This earned him the opportunity to speak at various meetings in England. He was selected fellow of the Royal Photographic Society; he was the second Indian to earn this distinction. Back home in 1913, he took over his father's enterprise called U Roy and Sons.

Sukumar Roy was a versatile genius. He used to compose rhymes at an early age. Along with photography he learnt painting. While at college, he used to write comedies and act in them. He also acted in a play called 'Goday Galad' with Rabindranath Tagore and Abanindranath Tagore at Santiniketan. He composed some songs during the Swadeshi Movement and also sang the songs himself. After his father's death, he took over the *Sandesh,* a magazine published by his father. While in England, he sent stories, poems and paintings to be published in the magazine.

While studying at Presidency College, he set up an organisation called 'Nonsense Club' and published the magazine *Sade-Batrish-Bhaja* as its mouthpiece. On his return from England, he started the Monday Club where he used to arrange discussions along with refreshments, which earned the club another name, Monda (Bangla for sweetmeat) Club.

Sukumar Roy was principally noted for his writings for young children. He mixed comic elements and subtle satire in all his works - poems, plays, stories or paintings. His satire is marked by his social consciousness. His prominent writings include, *Ha-Ya-Ba-Ra-La* (Topsy-Turvy, 1928), *Pagla Dashu* (1940), *Bahurupi* (The Jester, 1944), *Khaikhai* (I Want More, 1950), *Abak Jalpan* (Strange Drink), *Shabda Kalpadrum* (The Tree of Words) and *Jhalapala* (Irritation). He also wrote some serious essays in Bangla and English. He wrote a collection of belles-lettres called *Hesoramer Dairi,* written in the form of a diary.

Sukumar Roy's finest work *Abol-Tabol,* the nearest English translation of which can be 'nonsense' or 'gibberish,' was written in the last two and a half years of his life. He died in 1923, nine days before his best-loved book *Abol Tabol* was published. Anyone who has had his early schooling in Bengal, has grown up with the delightfully crazy verses of *Abol Tabol* that children love to recite. The poems of *Abol Tabol* had been gathered out of various issues of the children's magazine, *Sandesh,* which Sukumar Roy had been editing. The comic fantasies of *Abol Tabol* display a special brand of anarchic madness which bears the distinctive stamp of

Sukumar Roy. Among his fantastic characters is an old man who survives on boiled wood and can tell you the taste and smell of different kinds of wood ("Kaath Buro"). There is the old woman whose rickety house has been put together with spit. There is a singer whose voice echoes from Delhi to Burma and makes animals faint. Roy's artistry and genius is best portrayed in this collection of fine verses and if he had not written a single word elsewhere - *Abol Tabol* would have anyways made him what he is today.

JAISHANKAR PRASAD

(30.01.1889 – 14.01.1937)

Jaishankar Prasad was born on January 30th, 1889. He was one of the most famous figures in modern Hindi literature. He was a dramatist, novelist, poet and story-writer. Prasad belonged to the Chhayavadi school of Hindi poetry. His most famous work is *Kamayani*.

He was born in an elite family in Varanasi, Uttar Pradesh, India. His father Babu Devki Prasad, also known as Sunghani Sahu, was a tobacco dealer. He lost his father at an early age. He had to encounter some family problems at a relatively young age. However, he remained interested in literature, language, and history from his childhood days. He had a special inclination towards the Vedas. These interests are reflected in many of his works. He was also interested in the study of ancient relics. Apart from being a poet, he was also a philosopher, historian and a sculptor. In later years he made himself aloof from worldly matters, and adapted a nearly ascetic life. Though, some of his interests such as chess, gardening, *shashtrarth* and poetry-recitation remained with him.

His initial poetry (*Chitradhar* collection) was done in the Braj dialect of Hindi, but later he switched on to the Khadi Boli dialect or Sanskritized Hindi.

In his earlier days, he was influenced by Sanskrit dramas, but later the influence of Bengali and Persian dramas is evident on his works. Prasad's most famous dramas include *Skandagupta, Chandragupta* and *Dhruvaswamini*.

He is considered one of the four pillars of Chhayavad in Hindi literature along with Sumitranandan Pant, Mahadevi Verma and Suryakant Tripathi 'Nirala'. His style of poetry can at best be described as subtle. Art and philosophy has been exquisitely amalgamated in his writings. He used mainly Tatsam and Tatdbhav words - some of them made really exquisitely by himself.

The subject of his poetry spans the entire horizon of subjects of his era, from romantic to nationalistic. He in a way signifies the epitome of classical Hindi poetry. One of his patriotic poems, 'Himadri Tung Shring Se', won him many accolades in the era of Indian independence movement. However, *Kamayani* undoubtedly remains his best creation.

Kamayani is widely considered the best of his works. Majority of critics agree that it is the best work of poetry in Hindi. Though *Kamayani* has portrayals of divergent subjects, in entirety, it depicts the development of human culture in metaphoric style. *Kamayani* tells the story of the great flood and the central characters of the epic poem are Manu (a male) and Shraddha (a female). Manu is representative of the human psyche and Shraddha represents love. Another female character is Ida, who represents rationality. Some critics surmise that the three lead characters of *Kamayani* symbolise a synthesis of knowledge, action and desire in human life.

His dramas are considered to be the most pioneering ones in Hindi. Majority of them revolve around historical stories of ancient India. Some of them were also based on mythological plots.

He wrote short stories as well. The subjects were mixed - ranging from historical and mythological to contemporary and social. 'Mamta' (motherly love) is a famous short story based on an incident where a Mughal Badshah gets refuge in a Hindu widow's home whose father was killed by Badshah's army. Another one of his well-known short-stories called 'Chhota Jadugar' (little magician) portrays the life of a child who learns to earn his own living by performing small skits with his dolls on streets.

He also wrote a small number of novels.

PEARL S. BUCK

26.06.1892 – 06.03.1973

One of the most popular American authors of her day, humanitarian, crusader for women's rights, editor of *Asia Magazine*, philanthropist, noted for her novels of life in China, Pearl S. Buck was awarded the Nobel Prize for Literature in 1938.

Pearl S. Buck was born in Hillsboro, West Virginia, on 26 June, 1892. She spent her youth in China, in Chinkiang on the Yangtse river. She learned to speak Chinese before she could speak English. Her parents were missionaries. Buck's father, Absalom Sydenstricker, was a humourless, scholarly man who spent years translating the Bible from Greek into Chinese. Her mother, the former Caroline Stulting, had travelled widely in her youth and had a fondness for literature. Buck's life in China was not always pleasant. When she was only a child, the family was forced to flee from the rebel forces of the Boxer Rebellion.

After being educated by her mother and by a Chinese tutor, who was a Confucian scholar, Buck was sent to a boarding school in Shanghai (1907-09) at the age of fifteen. She also worked for the Door of Hope, a shelter for Chinese slave girls and prostitutes. Buck continued her education in the United States at Randolph-Macon Women's College in Virginia, where she studied psychology. After graduating in 1914, she returned to China as a teacher for the Presbyterian Board of Missions.

As a writer Buck started with the novel *East Wind: West Wind* (1930), which received critical recognition. She had earlier published autobiographical writings in magazines and a story entitled 'A Chinese Woman Speaks' in the *Asia Magazine.* Her breakthrough novel, *The Good Earth,* appeared in 1931. Its style, a combination of biblical prose and the Chinese narrative saga, increased the dignity of its characters. The book gained a wide audience, and was made into a motion picture.

In 1936 Buck was made a member of the National Institute of Arts and Letters. She became in 1938 the third American to win the Nobel Prize in Literature, following Sinclair Lewis and Eugene O'Neill. In 1951 she was elected to the American Academy of Arts and Letters. During World War II she lectured and wrote on democracy and American attitudes toward Asia.

It has been said that Buck introduced the theme of women's corporality into 20th century literature. Another major theme was interracial love. Through her personal experiences, Buck had much first-hand knowledge of the relationships between men and women from different cultures. In *The Hidden Flower* (1952) a Japanese family is overset when the daughter falls in love with an American soldier. *The Angry Wife* (1949) was about the love of Bettina, a former slave, and Tom, a southerner who fought for the army of the North. She died on 6 March, 1963.

SURYAKANT TRIPATHI 'NIRALA'

21.02.1896–15.10.1961

Suryakant Tripathi 'Nirala', one of the most significant poets of modern Hindi, was born on February 21, 1896 in a Brahmin family of Midnapore in Bengal (originally from Unnao, Uttar Pradesh). Though a student of Bengali, Nirala took keen interest in Sanskrit from the very beginning. In time, through his natural intelligence and acquired knowledge, he became an authority on various languages – Bengali, English, Sanskrit, and Hindi.

Nirala's life, barring short periods, was one long sequence of misfortunes and tragedies. His father, Pandit Ramsahaya Tripathi, was a government servant and a tyrannical person. His mother died when he was very young. Nirala was educated in the Bengali medium. However, after passing matriculation, he continued his education at home by reading Sanskrit and English literature. Thereon he shifted to Lucknow and then to village Gadhakola of District Unnao, to which his father originally belonged. Growing up, he took inspiration from personalities like Sri Ramakrishna Paramahansa, Swami Vivekananda and Rabindranath Tagore.

After his marriage at a young age, Nirala learnt Hindi at the insistence of his wife, Anohar Devi. Soon, he started writing poems in Hindi, instead of Bengali. After a bad childhood, Nirala had few good years with his wife. But this phase was short-lived as his wife died, when he was 20, and later his daughter, who was a widow, also expired. He also went through a financial crunch. During this phase, he worked for many publishers, worked as proof-reader and also edited *Samanvaya*.

Most of his life was somewhat in the Bohemian tradition. Since he was more or less a rebel, both in form and content, acceptance did not come easily. What he got in plenty was ridicule and derision. All this must have played a role in making him a victim of schizophrenia in his later life. He wrote strongly against social injustice and exploitation in the society.

Nirala died in Allahabad on 15 October, 1961. The world of Hindi literature is remarkable for ideological and aesthetic divisions. But today, the same reviled Nirala is one of the very few people in Hindi literature who are admired and respected by almost all, across all divisions. He amalgamated Vedanta, nationalism, mysticism, and love for nature and progressive humanist ideals in his works. The sources of his themes include history, religion, nature, Puranas and contemporary social and political questions.

He initiated the use of blank verse in his poems. He introduced aesthetic sense, love of nature, personal viewpoint and freedom of form and content in writing which went on to become the chief tenets of Chhayawad. His multifaceted genius, which ushered in a new style of poetry, acquired him the pseudonym, Nirala (unique). His poem 'Saroj Smriti' is one of the greatest, showing his emotions and sentiments for his daughter. Nirala is also credited with bringing in free verse in modern Hindi prose.

NIRAD C. CHAUDHURI

23.11.1897 – 01.08.1999

Nirad C. Chaudhuri was India's most distinguished writer of English prose in the 20th century. He was also perhaps his country's most controversial commentator since Independence: a lonely position he never regretted, maintained with real courage and indeed grew to relish. Throughout his immensely long life, which began in Bengal in the year of Queen Victoria's Diamond Jubilee, the physically diminutive Chaudhuri was fiercely independent of received opinion; his energy, analytical power and impatience with cant were the antithesis of the oriental stereotypes he confronted in his dozen or so books in English and Bengali.

His first and justifiably most famous book, *The Autobiography of an Unknown Indian*, a memoir of his childhood and youth, was described by V.S. Naipaul as "maybe the one great book to have come out of the Indo-British encounter" (thus dismissing Kipling and Forster). Its much-quoted dedication page shows how deliberate was Chaudhuri's occidental orientation and how he loved to provoke. It read: "To the memory of the British Empire in India which conferred subjecthood on us but withheld citizenship; to which yet every one of us threw out the challenge: 'Civis Britannicus sum' because all that was good and living within us was made, shaped and quickened by the same British rule."

Published in London in 1951, when India was in its first flush of freedom, the book infuriated many Indians, particularly the official class. "The wogs took the bait and having read only the dedication sent up a howl of protest," commented Chaudhuri's friend, the editor, historian and novelist Khushwant Singh. Chaudhuri was effectively forced out of government service, deprived of his pension and virtually blacklisted as a writer in India for some years.

But as more thoughtful Indian readers realised, even in the 1950s, and especially later, the *Autobiography* is actually a heartfelt, often wonderfully lyrical pleading on behalf of the best in Bengal: anti- nationalistic, but patriotic in the manner of, say, Alan Paton's *Cry the Beloved Country*. Chaudhuri's restless intelligence and extraordinarily wide learning in Bengali, Sanskrit and European (notably British and French) culture, could not allow him to fudge his growing conviction that Indians, particularly Bengalis, were failing to maintain the intellectual and moral standards set by their predecessors in the 19th century, and that independent India was heading for disaster.

In Delhi, during the 1947 partition, Chaudhuri had witnessed the riots, and the memory had seared his mind. "Political independence arrived for the Indian people on 15 August 1947. For a whole year before that they were engaged in making a red carpet for it to step on. It was dyed in the blood of hundreds of thousands of Indians who perished in the mass murders committed by the Hindus, the Muslims and Sikhs on one another," he wrote.

Nirad Chandra Chaudhuri was born in a Hindu family in 1897 in a small town in riverine East Bengal (now Bangladesh), where he was surrounded by religious rituals. His father, a lawyer of considerable breadth of mind, was however distinctly unorthodox, and by the time Nirad was in his late teens, he had freed his mind from orthodox Hindu beliefs and developed a passion for England and

English literature (though he was almost 60 before he visited Britain). But this early religious immersion would enable him to write, when he was 80, his iconoclastic *Hinduism* (1979) – a book disliked by scholars but arguably the most personally informed, accessible and honest summary of that multifarious religion.

Like most Bengalis of his time, Chaudhuri moved to Calcutta for his higher education, but soon found himself incapable of the sustained application required for a university degree; he failed to achieve the brilliant result he deserved. Instead he drifted into unsuitable work as a government clerk, followed by editorial attachments to leading Calcutta magazines.

These were years of penury and reflection that he recounts compellingly in his second, monumental volume of autobiography, *Thy Hand, Great Anarch!* (1987), published in his 90th year. What little money he had, he spent on books – including luxury editions – and on Western classical recordings, becoming one of the first Bengalis to appreciate such music seriously.

At last, aged 39, he was appointed for four turbulent years, 1937-41, as secretary to a well-known Bengali politician, the elder brother of Subhas Chandra Bose who had led the Indian National Army against the British in the Second World War (soldiers despised by Chaudhuri, who was an avid military historian, as turncoats and incompetent tacticians).

Here he enjoyed a ringside seat from where he could observe the maneuverings of Indian National Congress politicians before they obtained absolute power in 1947, and it set the seal on his antipathy for Indian nationalism and for some aspects of Gandhi. This did not prevent him, though, from swallowing his reservations and writing a mainly flattering, if premature obituary of the fasting Mahatma in 1943 while working for All India Radio in New Delhi - where he had recently shifted with his long-suffering, devoted wife Amiya and young family, abandoning Calcutta physically, though never mentally, for ever.

Gandhi survived, but his obituary, Chaudhuri discovered, had not survived the scrutiny of his Indian superiors who had deleted all the laudatory references. Five years later, after Independence, when Gandhi was assassinated, the obituary was finally broadcast - now with the deleted passages restored by the very same officials.

One can understand the contempt aroused in Chaudhuri by many such incidents, which he expressed in his prize-winning *The Continent of Circe* (1965). From the 1950s, and especially after 1970, when he and his wife settled in Oxford, he increasingly turned his fire upon modern Britain too, always with wit and sometimes with accuracy, in articles for British newspapers and periodicals, and asides in books such as *A Passage to England* (1959) and *Clive of India* (1975). Not that earlier he had endorsed the bulk of British policies and racial behaviour in India - as opposed to the beneficent influence of British (and other European) literature and thought - but the post-war British struck him as going rapidly and willingly into decline.

His final work in Bengali was a last effort to alert Bengalis to the real worth of Tagore, a giant writer and human being for Chaudhuri whom, he said with satirical truth, Bengalis were treating as "the holy mascot of Bengali provincial vanity". Like Tagore, Chaudhuri never quite lost the desire to appeal to his countrymen: he was always, as he once gleefully said, a bestseller among those who most reviled him.

THORNTON WILDER

17.04.1897 – 07.12.1975

American writer and playwright, best known for the Pulitzer Prize awarded play *Our Town* (1938). Wilder's breakthrough novel was *The Bridge of San Luis Rey* (1927), an examination of justice and altruism. The story focused on the fates of five travellers in the 18th century Peru, who happen to be crossing the finest bridge in the land when it breaks and throws them into the gulf below. A scholarly monk, Brother Juniper, interprets the story of each victim in an attempt to explain the working of divine providence. Surely, he argues, if there were any plan in the universe at all, if there were any pattern in human life, it could be discovered mysteriously latent in the lives of those particular people. But his book being done the text is pronounced heretical and both Juniper and his work are burned by the Inquisition.

"But soon we shall die and all memory of those five will have left earth, and we ourselves shall be loved for a while and forgotten. But the love will have been enough; all those impulses of love return to the love that made them. Even memory is not necessary for love. There is a land of the living and a land of the dead and the bridge is love, the only survival, the only meaning." (from *The Bridge of San Luis Rey*)

Thornton Wilder was born in Madison, Wisconsin, one of five children of Amos Parker Wilder, a newspaper editor, diplomat, and a strict Calvinist, and Isabella (Niven) Wilder, daughter of a Presbyterian minister. Embracing the Puritan heritage of his family, Wilder said later that "I don't think there's any doubt that the New England tradition is the highest point to which civilization culture ever attained.... My father, for all his faults, was the personification of the tradition."

In 1906 the family moved to Hong Kong, where his father had been appointed American Consul General. After six months Wilder's mother returned with her four children to the United States, but the family rejoined again in 1911 in Shanghai, where his father had been transferred. Wilder stayed in China for a year.

In 1915 Wilder enrolled in Oberlin College, where he studied the Greek and Roman classics in translation. The family moved in 1917 to New Haven, Connecticut, and Wilder entered Yale University. His first full-length play, *The Trumpet Shall Sound,* appeared in 1920 in the *Yale Literary Magazine,* but it was not produced until 1926 by the American Laboratory Theatre.

During WW I Wilder served for eight months in the Coast Artillery Corps as a corporal. He received his B.A. from Yale University in 1920, and went to Rome, where he studied archaeology at the American Academy. While teaching French at the Lawrenceville School in New Jersey, Wilder continued to write. By 1926 he had received an M.A. degree in French literature from Princeton University. In the same year appeared his first novel, *The Cabala,* a fantasy about a young American visiting Rome, where he meets a group of Italian aristocrats, who turn out to be incarnations of the ancient Roman gods.

Although Wilder had set the events of *The Bridge of San Luis Rey* in Peru, it was not until 1941, when he visited the country. With the success of this 34,000 word novella, Wilder could afford to resign his position at Lawrenceville. From 1930 to 1937 Wilder was a part-time lecturer in comparative literature at the University of Chicago, in 1935 he was a visiting professor at the University of Hawaii, Honolulu, and in 1950-51 a professor of poetry at Harvard University, Cambridge, Massachusetts.

Wilder's later plays are darker in tone. His oldest sister Charlotte, a poet, was institutionalized for mental illness in 1941, and his mother died in 1946. To his friends Wilder murmured that his own life had been a failure. And it has also been suggested that Wilder was denied the Nobel Prize because he was - wrongly - accused of plagiarizing *The Skin of Our Teeth* from Joyce's *Finnegans Wake.* Wilder wrote in the 1950s *The Wreck of the 5:25* (1957), *Bernice* (1957), and *Alcestiad,* based on Euripide's *Alcestis,* and performed at the Edinburgh Festival under the title of *Life in the Sun.* When Montgomery Clift criticized its dialogue as forced and pedantic, Wilder became, according to the actor, so enraged, that "he almost jumped into the Atlantic Ocean." *The Merchant of Younkers* (1938), a farce which had failed critically and commercially, was revised under the new title of *The Matchmaker* (1954). Wilder had based his earlier work on a British play called *A Day Well Spent* by John Oxenford. Later *The Matchmaker* served as the source for the Broadway musical *Hello, Dolly!,* which opened in 1964 in New York, starring Carol Channing and music and lyrics by Jerry Herman.

SUBHADRA KUMARI CHAUHAN

1904 – 15.02.1948

Subhadra Kumari Chauhan was a prominent poetess in India, whose writings used to be very emotionally charged. She was born in 1904 at Nihalpur village in Allahabad district. But after her wedding to Thakur Laxman Singh of Khandwa, Chauhan shifted to Jabalpur in the year 1919. Here, Subhadra Kumari Chauhan joined the famous non-cooperation movement launched by Mahatma Gandhi in 1921 and became the very first woman Satyagrahi in the country to court arrest at Nagpur.

In fact, she was put behind the bar twice because she dared to raise her voice against the British rule in India. Chauhan has also penned a plethora of works in Hindi poetry. Her most well-known composition is *Jhansi Ki Rani* narrating the life of the brave Jhansi Ki Rani Lakshmi Bai. Of the entire Hindi literature, it is this poem that's most recited and sung by the people of India. Some of her other famous poems include 'Veeron Ka Kaisa Ho Basant', 'Rakhi Ki Chunauti' and 'Vida'. These too explicitly talk about the freedom movement.

The poems and songs written by Subhadra Kumari Chauhan have served as a source of motivation for so many Indian youths to take part in Indian independence struggle. She predominantly used the simple and clear Khariboli dialect of Hindi in her writings. Other than these, Chauhan also used to write poems for children. She has penned many short stories based on the lifestyle of the middle-class

Indians. However, she died suddenly in a car accident in 1948.

Subhadra Kumari Chauhan was a distinguished Indian poetess, whose compositions used to be very emotionally charged. The government of India has named an Indian coast guard ship in her remembrance.

MULK RAJ ANAND

12.12.1905 – 28.09.2004

Mulk Raj Anand was born on December 12, 1905 in Peshawar. He graduated with honors from Khalsa College, Amritsar, in 1924. Mulk Raj Anand went to England and studied at University College 'London' and Cambridge University. He completed his Ph.D. in 1929. Mulk Raj Anand also studied - and later lectured - at League of Nations School of Intellectual Cooperation in Geneva. Between 1932 and 1945 he lectured intermittently at Workers Educational Association in London.

Mulk Raj Anand was initiated into the literary career by a family tragedy, instigated by the rigidity of the caste system. Anand's first prose essay was a response to the suicide of an aunt, who had been excommunicated by his family for sharing a meal with a Muslim. Mulk Raj Anand's first novel, *Untouchable* (1935), was a stark reflection of the day-to-day life of a member of India's untouchable caste. The book was widely acclaimed and Mulk Raj Anand was hailed as India's Charles Dickens. His second novel *Coolie* depicts the plight of India's poor through the story of a 15-year-old boy, trapped in servitude as a child labourer, who eventually dies of tuberculosis.

In the 1930s and 1940s Mulk Raj Anand divided his time between London and India. He joined the struggle for independence, but also fought with the Republicans in the Spanish Civil War. After the war Anand returned permanently to India and settled in Bombay (now Mumbai). In 1946 he founded the fine arts magazine *Marg*. He also became a director of Kutub Publishers. From 1948 to 1966 Anand taught at Indian universities. Mulk Raj Anand was fine art chairman at Lalit Kala Akademi (National Academy of Arts) from 1965 to 1970. In 1970, he became president of Lokayata Trust, for creating a community and cultural centre in the village of Hauz Khas, New Delhi.

Mulk Raj Anand was an Indian novelist, short-story writer. He was among the first writers to incorporate Punjabi and Hindustani idioms into English. Mulk Raj Anand's stories depicted a realistic and sympathetic portrait of the poor in India.

In *Two Leaves and a Bud* (1937) Anand continued his exploration of the Indian society. The story told about a poor Punjabi peasant. He is brutally exploited in a tea plantation and killed by a British official, who tries to rape his daughter. The socially conscious work shared much with the proletarian novels published in Britain and the United States during the 1930s.

Anand's famous trilogy, *The Village* (1939), *Across the Black Waters* (1940), and *The Sword and the Sickle* (1942), was a strong protest against social injustices. The story follows the life of Lai Sing from adolescent rebellion through his experiences in World War I, to his return home and revolutionary activities. In Anand's early novels his social and political analysis of oppression grows clearly from his involvement with the Left in England. Among Anand's later and most impressive works is *The Private Life of an Indian Prince* (1953). This time Anand focused more on human psyche and personal struggles than on class conflicts. The story had its origins in the betrayal of a hill-woman with whom the author was romantically involved while married to his first wife, the actress Kathleen van Gelder. Anand had met Gelder in London; they married in 1939.

After divorce in 1948, Anand married Shirin Vajifdar, a distinguished dancer. Anand's daughter from his first marriage became a writer, too. Since the 1950s, Anand intermittently worked on a projected seven-volume autobiography, entitled *Seven Ages of Man*. From the project appeared *Seven Summers* (1951), *Morning Face* (1968), *Confessions of a Lover* (1976), and *The Bubble* (1984). Anand also published books on subjects as diverse as Marx and Engels in India, Tagore, Nehru, Aesop's fables, the Kama Sutra, erotic sculpture, and Indian ivories. Mulk Raj Anand died in Pune on September 28, 2004. Along with the novelist and short story writer Munshi Premchand (1880-1936), Anand was involved in forming dalit literature, used to refer to the "untouchable", casteless sects of India.

JIM THOMPSON

27.09.1906 – 07.04.1977

James Meyers (Jim) Thompson was born in a jailhouse in Anadarko, Oklahoma. His father James Sherman Thompson, or "Big Jim," as he was called, was the town sheriff, a colorful figure. He foiled jail-breaks, rode with some of the most celebrated Western peace officers, and arrested horse thieves. He also was a chronic gambler and was in 1907 dismissed for misappropriating funds. Avoiding arrest, he fled to Mexico. For the next 14 years he travelled from one oil field to another with his family, and managed to acquire a fortune before going bankrupt. In 1921 he suffered a breakdown and died in an institution 20 years later.

Thompson received his B.A. from the University of Nebraska. He held numerous jobs – beginning as an oil well and pipeline worker. He became affiliated during the Depression with the Federal Writers Project in Oklahoma, helping to turn out guidebooks of the state. Thompson also contributed to "true crime" magazines. In this period, when trading in liquor was illegal, Thompson got to know the local gangsters, losers, deputies, corrupt civil servants, and later depicted their world in his books. In 1931 he married Alberta Thompson; they had two children. He also joined the Communist party and made friends with other political activists, such as folk singer Woody Guthrie.

Thompson had started writing for magazines in the 1920s, but in the 1940s he turned to crime fiction as a way of making money. Thompson's first novel, *Now and on Earth*

(1942), owed much to Erskine Caldwell and John Steinbeck. In it the father of the protagonist dies in an asylum, killing himself by eating the stuffing from his mattress, the fate Thompson often claimed of his own father. In 1946 *Heed the Thunder* appeared. These early books were not successful.

Thompson worked as a journalist for the *New York Daily News* and for the *Los Angeles Times Mirror*. In the 1950s he was blacklisted during the period of Joseph McCarthy's "crusade" against Communists. Later he was summoned to Hollywood by the director Stanley Kubrick to co-write screenplays. *The Killing* (1956), based on Lionel White's *Clean Break,* was a downbeat movie about robbery at a racetrack. Kubrick showed in it his characteristic precision and care in the construction. Sterling Hayden plays Johnny Clay who plans the robbery, but in the end most of his gang is shot and he loses the money.

Paths of Glory (1957) was an anti-war film based on Humphrey Cobb's 1935 novel. The story was set in the French trenches of World War I, starring Kirk Douglas and Adolphe Menjou. Kubrick rewrote the script with Thompson. Douglas considered it a catastrophe and he demanded that they use the original script, which was done. However, Thompson stayed in Hollywood and made scripts for the TV series 'Dr. Kildare and Convoy' and produced one paperback novel based on *Ironside*. Two years before his death Thompson had a cameo-appearance as Judge Grayle in the 1975 film adaptation of *Chandler's Farewell, My Lovely,* starring Robert Mitchum.

In the 1950s Thompson wrote nearly 20 novels, without much attempt at polishing them. He was frequently broke, regularly fired for his boozing, and sometimes separated from his family. His problems with liquor Thompson depicted in *The Alcoholics* (1953). Also *The Nothing Man* portrayed the victims of drink. Because of moderate success he wrote fast, and repeated himself in later works, recycling amongst others *The Killer Inside Me* again in *Pop. 1280* (1964). The awarded mystery writer and critic H.R.F. Keating selected it for his list of the one hundred best crime novels. "The great merit of the novels of Jim Thompson is that they are completely without good taste, and of them perhaps *Pop. 1280* (the title refers to the population of a small town in an imaginary Potts County in deepest America) has the least good taste of all." (Keating in *Crime & Mystery: the 100 Best Books,* 1987) In the story Nick Corey is seemingly a weak sheriff, but he eventually shoots one of his tormentors. When he kicks him he comments "It wasn't real nice to kick a dying man, and maybe it wasn't. But I'd been wanting to kick him for a long time, and it just never had seemed safe till now."

Thompson in the 1970s had several apoplectic strokes. He was always in need of money, and he drank it away as soon as he got any. In his last book, *King Blood* (1973) he returned to the figure of his father, "a heavyset young man with the profile of McKinley". Thompson died in Los Angeles on April 7, 1977. His death caused little attention and none of his work was in print at that time in his own country. Thompson remained in the U.S. a minor figure in the history of pulp fiction until some academic critics and publishers resurrected his work. His dialogue was seen as crisp as Hammett's, prose as convincing as Chandler's. Most of his novels and some of his uncollected short fiction have been reprinted.

R. K. NARAYAN

10.10.1906 – 13.05.2001

R.K. Narayan was born on October 10, 1906 in Madras. His father was a provincial headmaster. R.K. Narayan spent his early childhood with his maternal grandmother, Parvathi, in Madras and used to spend only a few weeks each summer visiting his parents and siblings. R.K. Narayan studied for eight years at Lutheran Mission School close to his grandmother's house in Madras, also for a short time at the CRC High School. When his father was appointed headmaster of the Maharaja's High School in Mysore, R.K. Narayan moved back in with his parents. He obtained his bachelor's degree from the University of Mysore.

R.K. Narayan began his writing career with *Swami and Friends* in 1935. Most of his work including *Swami and Friends* is set in the fictional town of Malgudi which captures everything Indian while having a unique identity of its own. R.K. Narayan's writing style was marked by simplicity and subtle humour. He told stories of ordinary people trying to live their simple lives in a changing world.

R.K. Narayan's famous works include *The Bachelor of Arts* (1937), *The Dark Room* (1938), *The English Teacher* (1945), *The Financial Expert* (1952), *The Guide* (1958), *The Man-Eater of Malgudi* (1961), *The Vendor of Sweets* (1967), *Malgudi Days* (1982), and *The Grandmother's Tale* (1993).

R.K. Narayan won numerous awards and honours for his works. These include: Sahitya Akademi Award for *The Guide* in 1958; Padma Bhushan in 1964; and AC Benson

Medal by the Royal Society of Literature in 1980; R. K. Narayan was elected an honorary member of the American Academy and Institute of Arts and Letters in 1982. He was nominated to the Rajya Sabha in 1989. Besides, he was also conferred honorary doctorates by the University of Mysore, Delhi University and the University of Leeds.

R.K. Narayan is one of the most famous and widely read Indian novelists. His stories are grounded in a compassionate humanism and celebrate the humour and energy of ordinary life.

MAHADEVI VARMA

26.03.1907 – 11.11.1987

She is a well known Hindi poet of the Chhayavad generation, the times when every poet used to incorporate romanticism in their poetry. She is more often called the Modern Meera. Well, we are talking about the famous Mahadevi Varma, who achieved the Jnanpith Award in the year 1982.

Mahadevi was born in a family of lawyers in 1907 in Farrukhabad, Uttar Pradesh. She completed her education in Jabalpur, Madhya Pradesh. At the young age of nine in the year 1914, she was married to Dr Swarup Narain Varma. She lived with her parents till the time her husband completed his studies in Lucknow. It is during this period that Mahadevi pursued further education at the Allahabad University. She did her Masters in Sanskrit from there.

She met her husband for sometime in the princely state of Tamkoi around 1920. Thereafter, she moved to Allahabad to further her interest in poetry. Unfortunately, she and her husband mostly lived separately and were busy pursuing their individual interests. They used to meet occasionally. Her husband died in the year 1966. Then, she decided to permanently shift to Allahabad.

She was highly influenced by the values preached by the Buddhist culture. She was so much inclined towards Buddhism that she even attempted to become a Buddhist bhikshuni. With the establishment of Allahabad (Prayag) Mahila Vidyapeeth, which was primarily set up to impart cultural values to girls, she became the first headmistress of the institute. This famous personality died in 1987.

Mahadevi Varma is one amongst the other major poets of the Chhayavaadi school of the Hindi literature. She is the epitome of child prodigy. Not only she wrote fabulous poetry, but also made sketches for her poetic works such as *Deepshikha* and *Yama*. *Deepshikha* is one of the best works of Mahadevi Varma. She is also famous for her book of memoirs.

Her writings were well acclaimed and earned her an important position in the world of Hindi literature. She is believed to be one of the supporting pillars of the Chaayavad movement. Her amazing poetry collection *Yama* brought her the Gyanpeeth Award, the highest Indian literary award. In the year 1956, the Government of India honoured her by conferring the title of Padma Bhushan upon her. She was the first Indian woman to become a Fellow of the Sahitya Akademi in the year 1979.

HARIVANSH RAI BACHCHAN

27.11.1907 – 18.01.2003

Harivansh Rai Bachchan was born on November 27, 1907 and died on January 18, 2003. He was a Hindi poet.

He was born in an ordinary Kayasth family in a small town near Allahabad. He was called "Bachchan" at home, which means "child." He received his formal schooling in a municipal school and attended Kayasth Pathshala to learn Urdu, which was the family tradition so as to help getting jobs in courts. He completed his later education both at the Allahabad University and Banaras Hindu University. Since, he gave up his university education to participate in the great upsurge of nationalism that began in 1930.

Dr. Harivansh Rai Bachchan burst upon the horizon of Hindi poetry as a bright star in 1935 with his critically acclaimed *Madhushala*, a 142 verse piece, which many have compared to the brilliant *Rubaiyyat* of Omar Khayyam. He was to carve out another niche for himself decades later with his autobiography in four volumes, beginning with *Kya Bhoolun Kya Yaad Karoon* regarded till date as a literary masterpiece.

Realizing that this was not the path he wanted to follow, he went back to university. However, from 1941 to 1952 he taught in the English Department at the Allahabad University and after that he spent the next two years at Cambridge University doing his doctoral thesis on W.B. Yeats. It was then that he used 'Bachchan' as his last name instead of *Srivastav*. Harivansh Rai's thesis got him his

Ph.D. at Cambridge. He however is the second Indian to get his doctorate in English literature from Cambridge. After returning to India he again took to teaching and also served at All India Radio, Allahabad.

In 1955, Harivansh Rai shifted to Delhi to join the External Affairs Ministry as an Officer on Special Duty and during the period of 10 years that he served, he was also associated with the evolution of Hindi as the official language. He also enriched Hindi through his translations of major writings. As a poet he is famous for his poem *Madhushala* (a bar selling alcoholic drinks). Besides Omar Khayyam's Rubaiyat, he will also be remembered for his Hindi translations of Shakespeare's *Macbeth* and *Othello* and also the *Bhagvad Gita*. However in November 1984 he wrote his last poem *Ek November 1984* on Indira Gandhi's assassination.

He got married to Shyama, his first wife in 1926. She was just 14 years old. But she died 10 years later after suffering from a long spell of TB. Shortly after her death Harivansh Rai married Teji Suri in 1942. The birth of his two sons Amitabh and Ajitabh changed the course of his life as his days of hardship ended when both his sons did extremely well in their careers - Amitabh became a superstar and a multi-billionnaire and Ajitabh turned out to be a successful business magnate in England.

Harivansh Rai was nominated to the Indian Rajya Sabha in 1966 and received the Sahitya Akademi Award three years later. In 1976 he was honoured with the Padma Bhushan for his immense contribution to Hindi literature. He was also honoured with the Saraswati Samman, the Soviet Land Nehru Award and the Lotus Award of the Afro-Asian Writers' Conference, for his unique contribution to the world of letters. But if ever asked to introduce himself, he had a simple introduction: *Mitti ka tan, masti ka man, kshan bhar jivan – mera parichay.* (A body of clay, a mind full of play, a moment's life - that is me.).

Dr. Harivansh Rai Bachchan passed away on January 18, 2003, Dr. Bachchan was 94 years old and had been suffering from serious respiratory ailments.

However, the poetry of Harivansh Rai had brought range, delicacy of feeling, ruggedness, ease and strength to the romantic lyric. Being born in a family known for its scholarship in Persian and its devotion to Vaishnav faith, his poetry combines the best of Sanskrit and Persio-Arabic poetic traditions. He had set a model of lyricism in Hindi and his contribution in changing the temper, approach and style of poetry during the 30s has been very significant.

The varied influences of Kabir, Keats, Tagore and Omar Khayyam were evident throughout his poetry, as also a deep appreciation of Shakespeare. He had also translated sixty-four Russian poems into Hindi entitled 101 poems of W.B. Yeats. For his Hindi translation of Russian poems he was honourcd with Soviet Land Nehru Award in 1966.

ROBERT A HEINLEIN

07.07.1907 – 08.05.1988

Robert A. Heinlein was born in Butler, Missouri, into a family of seven children. He attended public school in Kansas City and graduated from Central High School in 1924. In 1929 he graduated from the U.S. Naval Academy at Annapolis, and served in aircraft carriers and destroyers. During this period, he married Leslyn McDonald. In 1934 he was invalided out for tuberculosis. Heinlein started to study physics at the graduate school of U.C.L.A. He left the school without completing his studies and worked in odd jobs in mining and real estate without real success.

At the age of thirty-two, he turned his hand to the writing of science fiction. Heinlein's first published stories appeared in action-adventure pulp magazine *Astounding Science Fiction* in 1939. It was edited by John W. Campbell, who has been credited with moving science fiction toward its modern form. Under his influence writers started to examine how technology might affect the everyday life of ordinary people and society in general.

Heinlein never got over his navy discharge. After the Japanese attack on Pearl Harbor, he tried to enlist but was rejected. During World War II years from 1943 Heinlein published no stories, but worked as an engineer at the Naval Air Experimental Station, Philadelphia. His first novel, *Rocket Ship Galileo* (1947) paved way to childrens' science fiction. After divorce he married in 1948 Virginia Doris Gerstenfeld. From 1947 to 1959 Heinlein produced sixteen novels.

Heinlein's early works emphasized adventure and were aimed at young readers. In 1959 he received the Boys' Clubs of America Book Award. In these novels Heinlein avoided open didacticism, although his young protagonists learned lessons in courage, tolerance, and military virtues during the course of the story. Often Heinlein's male protagonist has to go through rites of passage - he meets a guru or somebody who has superior wisdom, and after a period of learning he has to earn his place in a group and prove his skills. *Citizen of the Galaxy* (1957), dedicated to Fritz Leiber, was actually Oliver Twist in space. In the story a young boy, Thorby, is bought from an inter-galactic slave market by a mysterious beggar, a benefactor, who later turns out to be a secret agent. Thorby learns to speak Finnish and after all kinds of adventures, he turns out to be from a wealthy corporate family from the Earth.

From the late 1950s Heinlein started writing expressly for adults and deal with such topics as cloning, incest, religion, free love and mysticism. Heinlein's religious views were in direct opposition to the literal interpretation of biblical scripture: "The most preposterous notion that H. Sapiens has ever dreamed up is that the Lord God of Creation, Shaper and Ruler of all the Universes, wants the saccharine adoration of His creatures, can be swayed by their prayers, and becomes petulant if He does not receive flattery. Yet this absurd fantasy, without a shred of evidence to bolster it, pays all the expenses of the oldest, largest, and least productive industry in all history.

In *Starship Troopers* (1959) Heinlein showed his fascination with the glamour of high-tech weaponry. The book earned him again the prestigious Hugo Award. *Starship Troopers* first appeared in abridged form in *The Magazine of Fantasy and Science Fiction* in 1959. The hero is Juan "Johnnie" Rico, son of a wealthy merchant who has enlisted in the army to impress the beautiful Carmen. After tough training he joins Rasczack's Roughnecks to battle against the "Bugs", intelligent arthropods. Johnnie's mother is killed in a bombing, Carmen becomes a starship pilot, and their mutual friend Carl dies in a battle in Pluto. Heinlein's militaristic novel can be interpreted as an attack on corruption and distorted views of democracy – only those willing to sacrifice their lives for the state may govern and vote – but also as a conflict between individualism and collectivism: the social system of the Bugs represent "total communism", Heinlein's regular publisher, Scribner's refused to publish the book and it eventually appeared under the Putnam imprint.

Heinlein's short stories were independent of one another but related in the author's *Future History: 1951-2600* AD time line. Some of his characters periodically appear in different novels, among the Lazarus Long from *Methuselah's Children* (1958). In *Time Enough for Love* (1973) Lazarus has a number of sexual adventures, travels back in time, and has sex with his own mother. 'A "pacifist male" is a contradiction in terms. Most self-described "pacifists" are not pacifist; they simple assume false colors. When the wind changes, they hoist the Jolly Roger.' (from *Time Enough for Love,* 1973) The life of Maureen Johnson, Lazarus's mother, is dealt in *To Sail Beyond the Sunset* (1987). Nearly all of Heinlein's work fit into a specific time period within this larger scheme. The idea was later imitated by several writers, with considerable success by Poul Anderson and Larry Niven. Also Isaac Asimov developed a similar scheme, and claimed imaginative copyright on the imagined future.

RAMDHARI SINGH DINKAR

23.09.1908 – 24.04.1974

Ramdhari Singh 'Dinkar' was an Indian Hindi poet, essayist and academician, who is considered as one of the most important modern Hindi poets. Dinkar emerged as a rebellious poet with his nationalist poetry in pre-Independence days. His poetry exuded Veer Rasa, and he has been hailed as a Rashtrakavi (National poet) evoking the spirit of nationalism on account of his inspiring patriotic compositions. As a mark of respect for him, his portrait was unveiled in the Central Hall of Parliament of India by the Prime Minister of India, Dr. Manmohan Singh, on his centenary year, 2008.

Dinkar initially supported the revolutionary movement during the Indian Independence struggle, but later became a Gandhian. However, he used to call himself a 'Bad Gandhian' because he supported the feelings of indignation and revenge among the youth. In *Kurukshetra,* he accepts that the war is destructive, but says that it is necessary for the protection of freedom.

Dinkar was three times elected to Rajya Sabha, and he was the member of this house from April 3, 1952 CE to January 26, 1964 CE, and was awarded the Padma Bhushan in 1959.

During the Emergency, Jayaprakash Narayan had attracted a gathering of one lakh people at the Ramlila Ground and thunderously recited Rashtrakavi Ramdhari Singh Dinkar's wonderfully evocative poetry: *Singhasan Khaali Karo Ki Janata Aaati Hai.*

Dinkar was born in a poor Bhumihar Brahmin family in Simariya village of Begusarai district in Bihar. As a student,

Dinkar's favourite subjects were history, politics and philosophy. He studied Hindi, Sanskrit, Maithili, Bengali, Urdu and English literature. Dinkar was greatly influenced by Iqbal, Rabindranath Tagore, Keats and Milton. He had even translated works of Rabindranath Tagore from Bangla into Hindi.

Shri Ramdhari Singh 'Dinkar', called the "Rashtrakavi", evoked the spirit of nationalism on account of his inspiring patriotic composition.A philosopher-poet, Shri Dinkar rose upon the Hindi literary scene like the proverbial 'Sun'.

His works are mostly of 'Veer Rasa', or the 'brave mode'. *Urvashi*, of course, is an exception. Some of his greatest works are *Rashmirathi* and *Parashuram ki Prateeksha*. He is hailed as the greatest Hindi poet of 'Veer Rasa' since Bhushan.

Acharya Hazari Prasad Dwivedi wrote that he was very popular among people whose mother-tongue was not Hindi and he was a symbol of love for one's own mother-tongue. Harivansh Rai Bachchan wrote that for his proper respect he should get four Jnanpith Awards - for poetry, prose, languages and for his service to Hindi. Rambriksh Benipuri wrote that Dinkar is giving voice to the revolutionary movement in the country. Namvar Singh wrote that he was really the sun of his age.

Hindi writer Rajendra Yadav, whose novel *Sara Akash* also carried a few lines of Dinkar's poetry, has said of him: 'He was always very inspiring to read. His poetry was about reawakening. He often delved into Hindu mythology and referred to heroes of epics such as Karna. He was a poet of anti-imperialism and nationalism'.

He also wrote social and political satires aimed at socio-economic inequalities and exploitation of the underprivileged. He died on April 24 in 1974.

SAADAT HASAN MANTO

11.05.1912 – 18.01.1955

Saadat Hasan Manto was an acclaimed but a controversial South Asian literary figure. He was born in Sambrala, in the Ludhiana district of the Punjab in the year 1912. As a young man, Manto began his literary career with an Urdu translation of Victor Hugo's *The Last Days of a Condemned Man.* Going through his works it is pretty evident that during the starting of his career; Manto was deeply influenced by French and Russian realist writers such as Hugo, Anton Chekhov and Maxim Gorky. During the 1930s, Manto was also peripherally involved with the Indian Progressive Writers Association. IPWA was a left-leaning literary movement that was committed to the ideals of social uplift and justice through literature.

During his career, Manto wrote more than two hundred stories and a number of essays, film scripts, and radio plays. However, his greatest contributions to Indian literature were his mastery of the short story genre and his use of the Urdu language. Some of his well-known Urdu short stories include "Bu", "Khol Do", "Thanda Gosht", and "Toba Tek Singh," that were promptly translated into English after Manto's death.

After the partition of India, Manto left his home in Mumbai and migrated to Lahore, Pakistan, in January 1948. Although Manto's last years in Pakistan were filled with financial hardship and failing health, they were also instrumental in the compilation of some of his greatest literary achievements. Manto died of excessive drinking that led to liver cirrhosis, in the year 1955.

MICHAEL GILBERT

17.07.1912 – 08.02.2006

Michael Gilbert was born in Lincolnshire. He was educated at St. Peter's School, Seaford, Sussex, Blundell's School (1926-31), and at the University of London, attaining LL.B. with honors in 1937. For a short period he worked as a teacher in Salisbury.

Gilbert started to write in 1938, but the war intervened and his first book did not appear until 1947. During World War II he served in the Royal Horse Artillery in North Africa and Europe. He was captured in 1943 in North Africa and sent to a military prison near Parma in Italy. Gilbert managed to escape from the camp and this experience he later used in the novel *Death in the Captivity* (1952), which also inspired the film *Danger Within* (1959).

After the war Gilbert worked as a solicitor (1947-51), and became in 1952 a partner in the law firm of Trower, Still, and Kealing. In 1947 he married Roberta Marsden. During his early days as a London solicitor, Gilbert became legal adviser to Raymond Chandler. Gilbert retired from the firm in 1983.

Gilbert was a founding member of the British Crime Writers Association. In 1988 he was named a Grand Master by the Mystery Writers of America, and he won the Life Achievement Anthony Award at the 1990 Bouchercon in London. In 1980 Gilbert was made a Commander of the Order of the British Empire. Besides crime novels Gilbert wrote short stories and plays. The author's legal background contributed to his novels about law, young solicitors, and courtroom procedures. Gilbert also edited a book of legal anecdotes. He died on February 8, 2006, at his home in Luddesdown, Kent.

Several of his books Gilbert wrote on his 50-minute trip between his home in Kent and workplace in London. As a mystery novelist Gilbert made his debut with *Close Quarters* (1947). It introduced Inspector Hazelrigg, master of deduction, who is one of the earliest realistic British policemen in fiction. Hazelrigg has more than 30 years experience, he is red-faced and bulky, and has a cat in his office. Dedicated to his work, he appeared in several mysteries set in the London underworld, the Soho trattorias and nightclubs, and the gangland down by the docks. Hazelrigg also fought against fascist organizations.

Another of Gilbert's much-loved series' characters, the insomniac solicitor Henry Bohun, was introduced in the classic novel *Smallbone Deceased,* in which the remains of a law firm's client are found in a deed box. The book has one of the most eloquent depictions of intoxication in the mystery genre: "John had by now reached that well-defined stage in intoxication when every topic becomes the subject of exposing and generalisation, when sequences of thought range themselves in the speaker's mind, strewn about with flowery metaphor and garlanded in chains of pellucid logic; airborne flights of oratory to which the only obstacle is a certain difficulty with the palatal consonants." Bohun is excessively energetic and his background gives him many talents: he has been a medical student, an actuary, a research statistician, a soldier during WW II. Finally, he has chosen a legal career at the office of Horniman, Birley, and Crane, a respectably London firm. In *The Crack in the Teacup*

(1966) the hero was also a young solicitor and finds himself involved in a major campaign against racketeering. Bohun reappeared in several short stories, which were collected in *Stay of Execution* (1971).

In the postwar caper *The Doors Open* (1949), Gilbert made an excursion into the world of high finance. The book was written on a commuter train. In the story one of the protagonists, Paddy Yeatman-Carter, sees a man attempt suicide on a commuter train. When the man shows up dead the next day, Paddy and his friend Nap Rumbold, a lawyer, become suspicious of the dead man's employers, an insurance company.

Ellery Queen regarded *Game with our Rules* (1967) as one of "the best volumes of spy stories ever written." The book appeared in the ultra-heroic age of agent fiction, but reflected more the Kim Philby and Profumo spy scandals of 1950s and early 1960s Britain. The central characters are Daniel Calder, whose hobbies are firing small arms and playing the cello, and his friend Samuel Behrens, who is a specialist in European languages. They are gentleman spies, who operate mainly in England, and in most cases try to stop traitors from giving away secrets to the Soviets. One of the stories, 'Heilige Nacht,' took place in the divided Germany, the most popular scene of spy fiction. *The Night of the Twelfth* (1976) was partly based on Gilbert's experiences as a schoolmaster. The main plot concerns the torture and murder of schoolboys. Another plot deals with terrorists and their target, the son of the Israeli ambassador.

DYLAN THOMAS

27.01.1914 – 09.11.1953

Welsh poet and prose writer whose works are known for musical quality of the language, comic or visionary scenes and sensual images. Dylan Thomas died in the United States on a tour on November 9, 1953. His death resulted much from his alcoholism, which have gained mythic proportions. The Dylan Thomas Centre in Swansea even serves pints of Dylan's smooth ale. It has been claimed that the famous American songwriter and musician Bob Dylan, who was born Robert Allen Zimmerman, named himself after the Welsh poet, but Dylan himself had denied it.

"The hand that signet the paper felled a city;

Five sovereign fingers taxed the breath,

Doubled the globe of dead and halved a country;

These five kings did a king to death."

(from *The Hand That Signed the Paper*, 1936)

Dylan Thomas was born in the seaport town Swansea, West Glamorgan. His father, David John Thomas, was the senior English master at Swansea Grammar School, where Thomas was educated. His parents had a Welsh-speaking country background from Carmarthenshire, but they adopted English language and culture. Although Thomas could not speak Welsh, he picked up the rhythms of the language, and started to write poetry while still at school.

Thomas received little formal education. When he was twelve, his poem was published in the *Western Mail.*

Actually the work was copied from the *Boy's Own Paper*. Other verse, original without any doubts, he wrote for the *Grammar School Magazine*. Ignoring his father's advice to attend university, he left his studies and worked as a trainee newspaper reporter on the *South Wales Evening Post*. His first book, dreamlike and sensuous *18 Poems* (1934), marked the appearance of an energetic new voice in English literature. Thomas wrote the poems when he was nineteen and twenty years old. In 'I see the boys of summer' Thomas identifies himself with doomed Welshmen, victims of time. "Awake, my sleepers, to the sun, / A worker in the morning town, / And leave the poppied pickthank where he lies; / The fences of the light are down, / All but the briskest riders thrown, / And worlds hang on the trees."

The collection was followed by *Twenty-Five Poems* (1936), which established his reputation. Thomas moved to London where he worked as a broadcaster, prose writer, poet, and lecturer. With the writer Pamela Hansford Johnson, he started correspondence and a love affair. "Charming, very young-looking with the most enchanting voice," she wrote in her diary when they met. Later she married Lord C.P. Snow. In 1937 Thomas married Caitlin Macnamara, whom he called in a letter "Betty Boop". For a while the couple settled at Laugharne in Wales, returning there permanently after many wanderings in 1949. The marriage was stormy; Thomas was a natural bohemian and eventually Caitlin became tired in her husband's frecklessness. Thomas's earnings were irregular, his earnings just melted away, and he had to borrow money from his friends.

By the enu of the 1930s, Thomas had gained fame in the literary circles, but he also suffered from depression and was afraid of losing inspiration. He became later a highly admired public figure due to his radio work and readings. His romantic, rhetorical style won a large following. Some writers, among them Philip Larkin, rejected his work as too subjective.

Unfit for active service, Thomas worked during World War II as a documentary film script writer. With Alan Osbiston he directed the documentary 'These Are The Men' (1943), an attack on the Nazi leaders, which used shots from Leni Riefenstahl's 'The Triumph of the Will' (1935). Sporadically Thomas was employed by the BBC, where his striking, melodic voice made him a media star. After the German planes had firebombed London, Thomas composed the lines: "Deep with the first dead lies London's daughter, Robed in the long friends, / The grains beyond age, the dark veins of her mother, / Of the riding Thames. / After the first death, there is no other." (from 'A Refusal to Mourn the Death, by Fire, of a Child in London', 1946) In the 1940s Thomas wrote some of his best works. *Portrait of an Artist as a Young Dog* (1940) was a collection of largely autobiographical short stories, paying homage to James Joyce. *Deaths and Entrances* (1946) used religious imagery and took its subjects among others from the bombing of London, or from the loss of childhood world as in the poem 'Fern Hill'. Another pastoral ode, 'Poems in October,' expressed Thomas's nostalgia for lost youth.

In 1947, when Thomas contributed to more than 50 features for the BBC, he suffered a mental breakdown, and moved to Oxford. He returned to Wales in 1949 and made his first American tour next year, mostly because of financial pressures. In 1950, 1952, and 1953 Thomas continued his popular reading tours on American college campuses, managing to hide that he did not like reading his own work, but unable to resist the temptation to live up to his own reputation for being wild and drunken. Before a reading at Pomona College, Claremont, he lost his books and notes. In New York, he spent a lot of time at the Chelsea Hotel Bar. The tours were financially profitable and he met such celebrities as Greta Garbo, Marilyn Monroe, and Charlie Chaplin. At Chaplin's, he was seen urinating on a plant.

Thomas died at St. Vincent's Hospital, after spending four days in a coma. According to a story, he had boasted to his American girlfriend, Liz Reitell, that he had drunk 18 straight whiskies in a bar in Manhattan. At the hospital a doctor had given him various drugs and an injection of morphine. In spite of Thomas's heavy drinking, the autopsy revealed that he did not suffer from serious cirrhosis of the liver. Caitlin Macnamara Thomas died in 1994.

His last four years Thomas spent at the Boat House in Laugharne, where he later was buried. The cottage was purchased for the family by Margaret Taylor, the wife of the historian A.J.P. Taylor. Shortly before his death in New York, Thomas took part in a reading of what was to be his most famous single work. *Under Milk Wood* (1954) was a return to the Welsh landscape, and a celebration of domestic life and dreams of ordinary people. It was published posthumously as his reminiscence *A Child's Christmas in Wales* (1955). His *Notebooks* appeared in 1968. A new edition of *The Poems of Dylan Thomas* (1971) included personal comments by his friend and early collaborator, the composer Daniel Jones. The musician John Cale has set several of Thomas's poems to music. "As to the Thomas heritage industry: ouch!" Cale has said.

Thomas's poetry is marked by vivid metaphors, the use of Christian and Freudian imagery, and celebration of the mystical power of growth and death. "My poetry," Thomas once said, "is the record of my individual struggle from darkness toward some measure of light." Although Thomas's poems appear to be freely flowing, his work sheets reveal much work behind his mixture of the vernacular and literary. To Pamela Hansford Johnson he once said in the 1930s, that he wrote at the rate of two lines an hour. Among his best-known individual poems are 'And death shall have no dominion,' 'Altarwise by owllight' (a sonnet sequence), 'A Refusal to Mourn the Death, by Fire, of a Child in London,' 'Do not go gentle into that good night,' 'In My Craft and Sullen Art,' and 'Fern Hill.' His own role and gift as a poet Thomas paralleled with the forces of nature: "Oh as I was young and easy in the mercy of his means, / time held me green and dying / though I sang in my chains like the sea." (from 'Fern Hill')

LAURIE LEE

26.06.1914 – 13.05.1997

Laurie Lee was born in Stroud, Gloucestershire, where life had followed its traditional course for centuries. The families were large, they lived in overcrowded cottages; there were no modern conveniences and it was accepted as a normal pattern of life and death that many children died young. Lee's father lived in London and worked there as a civil servant – his first wife had died and he had married Lee's mother who took care of his two families and believed that one day he would return to her. Lee was educated at the village school and at Stroud Central School. When he was fifteen he left school and became an errand-boy. Lee also gave lectures on the violin.

In his teens Lee had already began to write poems. He had met two sisters who encouraged him in his writing aspirations. Both sisters were passionately involved with him. At the age of twenty Lee left for London, and worked for a year as a builder's labourer. He then spent four years travelling in Spain and the eastern Mediterranean. During these years he met a woman who helped him financially and sent him to university to study art.

Lee's first poem appeared in *Horizon* in 1940, and his first collection, *The Sun my Monument,* was published in 1944. Lee's romantic poems show the influence of Federico García Lorca. He has noted that his poems "were written by someone I once was and who is so distant to me now that I scarcely recognize him anymore." Several poems written in the early 1940s reflect the atmosphere of the war, but also capture the beauty of the English countryside.

With *A Rose for Winter* (1955) Lee started his autobiographical production. It tells of Lee's trip to Spain 15 years after his first visit, finding a country ravaged by war, but where people enjoyed bullfights and he could earn his living by playing the violin. *Cider with Rosie* (1959) focused with a series of sketches on the author's childhood in the Gloucestershire village Slad. Parts of the book were published earlier in the magazines *Orion, Encounter, The Queen, The Cornhill, Leader Magazine,* and *The Geographical.* The lyrical and sensuous work avoided social or political comments about the hardships of poverty, but presented a variety of memorable, temperamental figures, among them Lee's mother. Lee learns to play the violin, his sister Frances dies, and he has his first early, tentative sexual experiences at the age of 10-11 with Jo, and later with Rosie Burdock, with whom he drinks cider under a hay wagon, and is never the same again. Rosie's identity was kept secret for 25 years. She was in Rose Buckland, Lee's cousin by marriage.

In an interview the author later said that the book was not a novel and not an autobiography. "... it is not so much about me as about the world that I observed from my earliest years. It was a world that I wanted to record because it was such a miracle visitation to me. I wanted to communicate what I had seen, so that others could see it." (Laurie Lee in *The New York Times*, February 24, 1985) The memoir has sold more than six million copies. It was published by Chatto & Windus, and according to Diana Athill, "Laurie must already have been dabbling in the manipulative games with publishers that he was to play with increasing zest in the future..." (from *Stet: an Editor's Life* by Diana Athill, 2000)

As I Walked out One Midsummer Morning narrates Lee's first trip to Civil War Spain in 1936 and his walk across the country from Vigo to Granada. In Castillo he works in a hotel, but when the city is taken by Franco's troops, he returns to England, only to realize that the war is not over. *Two Women* (1983) was a story of Lee's courtship of his wife Cathy, and the birth and growth of their daughter Jessy. *A Moment of War* told of a young man's walk over the Pyrenees into Spain to fight in the International Brigades in 1937. Before joining the colorful company of volunteers from Russia, France, the United States, England, and other countries, he was arrested as a spy and imprisoned for some time.

KHUSHWANT SINGH

Born in 1915

Khushwant Singh is a senior prominent Indian novelist-cum-journalist. He was born on 2 February 1915 at Hadali in British India that is now a part of Punjab in Pakistan. A significant post-colonial writer in the English language, Khushwant Singh is known for his clear-cut secularism, humour and a deep passion for poetry. His assessment and comparison of social and behavioural traits of people from India and the West is full of outstanding wit.

Infact, Khushwant Singh's writing is so popular that his weekly newspaper column, "With Malice towards One and All", published in many Indian national dailies, is among the most widely-read commentaries in the country. Singh completed his bachelor's from the Government College at Lahore and thereafter, pursued further studies in law at King's College in London, UK. Sir Sobha Singh, Khushwant Singh's father, then used to work at a reputed builder in Lutyens' Delhi.

Once while still practicing as a lawyer in the High Court of Lahore, Khushwant Singh was on his way to his family's summer residence at Kasauli at the foothills of the Himalayas. It was just days prior to the partition of India and Pakistan in August 1947. Singh was driving his car when he came across a jeep full of Sikhs on an unusually vacant road that day. The Sikh men pridefully narrated to him how they had just butchered away all residents of a Muslim village.

All these instances found vivid description in the book *Train to Pakistan* Khushwant Singh later wrote in 1956. In the time to come, Singh was appointed to edit *Yojana,* a journal published by the Indian government. Other publications whose editing Singh was encharged with were the *Illustrated Weekly of India,* a newsweekly and two other major Indian dailies - *The National Herald* and the *Hindustan Times.* Under his leadership, *The Illustrated Weekly* came to be hailed as India's pre-eminent newsweekly.

There's many other kudos bagged by Khushwant Singh. For instance, Singh was a Rajya Sabha member of the Indian Parliament from 1980 to 1986. He was also honoured with the Padma Bhushan award in the year 1974 for service to his country, but he returned the award in protest against the siege of the Golden Temple by the Indian Army in 1984. Undeterred, the Indian government awarded Singh an even more prestigious honour, the Padma Vibhushan in the year 2007.

A significant post-colonial writer in the English language, Khushwant Singh is known for his clear-cut secularism, wit and a deep passion for poetry

JUDITH WRIGHT

31.05.1915 – 26.06.2000

Judith Wright, born in the early 20th century, was a well-known Australian poet, short-story writer and conversationalist. She was also a highly acclaimed critic of Australian poetry. Apart from this, Wright was an uncompromising campaigner for Aboriginal land rights. She had received honorary degrees from several universities and was also appointed as one of the members of Australia Council (in 1973-74).

Wright had written numerous poems, literary criticism and letters in her life and strongly believed the fact that a poet should be concerned with national and social problems. Her works have been awarded a number of times and translated into other languages also, like Italian, Japanese and Russian. Wright was also a highly successful literary critic and had edited several collections of Australian verse in her career.

Judith Wright was born on the 31st May, 1915, in Armidale, New South Wales, Australia. However, Wright spent most of her formative years in Brisbane and Sydney. She was the first child of Phillip Wright and his first wife, Ethel. When she was still in the tender years of her life, Wright went through frequent ill-health of her mother. This was when she started writing poetry, mainly to please her mother and bring her merriment.

Wright was brought up in her family's sheep station, until the death of her mother, in 1927. Thereafter, she was put under the guidance of her grandmother, who also took care of her education. In the year 1929, at the age of 14, Judith Wright enrolled in New England Girls School. Her love for poetry enhanced in the school, as it gave her immense comfort and solace. This was when she decided to become a poet.

In 1934, Judith Wright gained admission in Sydney University, where she studied philosophy, history, psychology and English, without taking a degree. At the beginning of World War II, the shortage of manpower brought Wright back to her father's station. This served as the turning point in her life, as she developed immense attachment to the land and its people. This love for people and land was visible in her works as well.

Wright, in her 20s, started becoming increasingly deaf. In 1937-38, she travelled to Britain and Europe. Until 1944, she worked as a secretary-stenographer and clerk. From the year 1944 to 1948, she worked at the University of Queensland, St. Lucia, as the university statistician. In 1946, she made her debut in poetry, with her first book *The Moving Image* being published. During this time, she also worked with Clem Christensen, editor of the literary journal *Meanjin*.

Judith Wright's meeting with J.P. McKinney, and moving to Queensland, proved beneficial to her career. She wrote most of her works in the mountains of southern Queensland only. Her next move, to Braidwood, was with respect to her protest against the political policies of Joh Bjelke-Petersen, the Premier of Queensland. It was here that Wright composed her nature-based poetry. Apart from being a poetess, Wright produced hack work, school plays for Australian Broadcasting Commission and children's books, to earn her livelihood.

Wright also lectured, as a part-timer, at various Australian universities. In 1975, all her addresses and speeches were collected in the literary criticism *Because I Was Invited*. Around this time, she was selected as a foundation fellow of the Australian Academy of the Humanities and an emeritus professor of the Literature Board of the Arts Council of Australia. Some time later, she wrote her own memoir, *Half a Lifetime*, covering her life until 1960s, which was published in 2000.

On 26th June, 2000, Wright died of a heart attack, in Canberra. At that time, she was 85 years old. Her ashes were scattered around the cemetery of Tamborine Mountain. Her possession of a strip of rainforest was donated to the state government, so it could be preserved as a national park.

Judith Wright's writing style was steeply inspired by the places in which she had stayed - New England, New South Wales, the subtropical rainforests of Tamborine Mountain, Queensland and the plains of the southern highlands (near Braidwood). For Wright, her mission was to connect the human experience with the natural world, through poetry and other works.

Land played an important and influential role for Judith Wright, all her life. This can widely be seen in her poetry, in which she takes effort to bridge the gap between nature and man. Wright condemned the educational system and blamed it for failing to teach the students the art and pleasure of poetry. On her part, she popularized poetry by promoting students to read and write poems in schools. However, she also expressed the uncertainty of poetry changing the scheme of things.

Judith Wright, together with David Fleay, Kathleen McArthur and Brian Clouston, was a founding member of the Wildlife Preservation Society of Queensland. She was also the President of the Society, from 1964 to 1976. She fought to conserve the Great Barrier Reef, when its ecology was threatened by oil drilling, and campaigned against sand mining on Fraser Island. Wright, along with her friends, founded one of the earliest nature conservation movements. She was also an ardent supporter of the Aboriginal land rights movement. Shortly before her death, she attended a march in Canberra, for reconciliation between white Australians and the Aboriginal people.

KAIFI AZMI

1919 – 10.05.2002

Born as Akhtar Hussain Rizvi in a family of landlords of a small town of Uttar Pradesh, Kaifi Azmi was a very renowned Urdu poet of India. Though his father, Syed Fateh Hussain Rizvi was a landlord, he also worked as a Tehsildar in a small state in Uttar Pradesh. The life history of Kaifi Azmi is absolutely inspiring and a glimpse of Kaifi Azmi biography will truly give you an idea as to what genius people are made of.

Kaifi Azmi's father wanted to send him to a school that imparted English education. Despite his best efforts, he could not do so because he faced stiff opposition from the elders of the family. Others wanted him to become a theologian and Kaifi Azmi was sent to a very reputed institution of Lucknow that was called Sultan al Madaris. Kaifi Azmi was a radical thinker and this created many problems for the institution. He was instrumental in creating a Student's Union and asked every student to go on strike to get their demands fulfilled. The college authorities were provoked and they expelled Kaifi Azmi out of the college.

Though he could not become a theologian, he got many degrees in different languages and mastered languages like Arabic, Urdu and Persian. He also passed various examinations from the university of Allahabad. Many great writers of Lucknow noticed him and they gave him constant encouragement and support. He started to rise up on the ladder of poetry and rapidly gained fame and recognition. He began from a very tender age of 11. His initiation into poetry has an interesting story behind it.

He managed to get himself invited to a Mushaira (poetry recital event) once. Over there, he recited a couplet, which was very much appreciated by everyone present there. When the news reached his father, he said that Kaifi must have recited his brother's ghazal. But when his brother denied it, people were very fascinated by this young protégé. With his poetry, he also joined the communist party during the Quit India Movement for Independence.

He left his comfortable life and worked in the textile mills of Kanpur. All this, at a young age of 24. He was required to shift to Bombay (now Mumbai) and work there for his party. At the same time, he was asked to attend Mushairas every now and then in different parts of the country. There he met fall in love with and married a woman named Shaukat. Shaukat Kaifi went on to become a famous theatre artist and also worked in films.

As a ghazal writer, Kaifi Azmi used a lot of romance and love in his poetry. But as he evolved into much more serious forms of writing, he started to write on the disturbances in the society and what the common man was going through. His poetry began to make people socially aware of their surroundings. He highlighted exploitation of the poor and generated much sympathy for the downtrodden section of the society. His poetry has a powerful and intense form of emotional compassion. His poems are famous for rich imagery and his contribution in the field of Urdu poetry is immense. He has won many awards and has also tried his hand at films and acting. He expired on May 10th, 2002, after a series of cardiac problems.

R. K. LAXMAN

Born in 1920

R. K. Laxman was born (1920) in Mysore in a Tamil family, in the state of Karnataka. His father was a headmaster and Laxman is the youngest of six boys. One of his elder brothers, R.K. Narayan, went on to become one of India's best known English language novelists.

Laxman was the captain of his local "Rough and Tough and Jolly" cricket team and his antics inspired the stories "Dodu the money maker" and "The Regal Cricket Club" written by his brother, Narayan. Laxman's idyllic childhood was shaken for a while when his father suffered a paralytic stroke and died around a year later, but the elders at home bore most of the increased responsibility, while Laxman continued with his schooling.

After high school, Laxman applied to the JJ School of Arts, Bombay, hoping to concentrate on his lifelong interests of drawing and painting, but the dean of the school wrote to him that his drawings lacked, "the kind of talent to qualify for enrolment in our institution as a student," and refused admission. He finally graduated with a Bachelor of Arts from the University of Mysore. In the meantime he continued his freelance artistic activities and contributed cartoons to *Swarajya* and an animated film based on the mythological character, Narada.

Laxman's earliest work was for newspapers and magazines such as *Swarajya* and *Blitz*. Whilst still at the Maharaja's College, Mysore, he began to illustrate his elder brother R K Narayan's stories in *The Hindu*, and he drew political cartoons for the local newspapers and for the *Swatantra.* Laxman also drew cartoons, for the Kannada humour magazine, *Koravanji.* Incidentally, *Koravanji* was founded in 1942 by Dr M Shivaram. He was a MBBS doctor, who had a clinic around Majestic area in Bangalore. He started this monthly magazine, dedicating to hilarious/ satiric articles and cartoons. He encouraged Laxman quite a lot. He held a summer job at the Gemini Studios, Madras. His first full-time job was as a political cartoonist for the *Free Press Journal.* Prominent Shiv Sena politician Bal Thackeray, was also an employee at the newspaper at that time. Laxman later joined *The Times of India,* beginning a career that has spanned for over fifty years.

JAMES JONES

06.11.1921 – 09.05.1977

James Jones was born in Robinson, Illinois, the son Ramon Jones, a dentist, and Ada Blessing Jones. His grandfather owned one of the oldest and biggest houses on East Main Street. Jones's father had problems with alcohol, he had a reputation as the town drunk, but there was a strong affection between the father and the son. Jones completed his high school education in Illinois, but because the family had gone broke during the Depression, he couldn't continue studies. While in Hawaii, Jones's mother died, and a year later his Jones's father committed suicide with a pistol; he shot himself two times in the head.

During World War II Jones served in the US army as a sergeant (1939-44). During this period he wrote several letters to his brother Jeff, who shared his literary aspirations – the letters were later published in To Reach Eternity (edited by George Hendrick, 1989). Jones was at Pearl Harbor when the Japanese attacked; on Guadalcanal he was injured in a combat, and received the Bronze Star and a Purple Heart. He also boxed as a welterweight in Golden Gloves tournaments. Jones's boxing career gave much authentic flavour to the fight scenes in From Here to Eternity. To make up for his lack of higher education, Jones attended the University of Hawaii for a short time in 1942 while stationed on Oahu. In 1945 he attended New York University.

Jones's wartime experiences in Hawaii formed the background for his first novel, *From Here to Eternity,* which depicted life in an Army base at the time of Pearl Harbour.

Jones spent six years writing the book. The beauty and power of the narrative gained acclaim among critics and readers. It became a Book of the Month Club selection and received the National Book Award for fiction in 1951. The central character of the story is Private Robert E. Lee Prewitt, a recruit from Kentucky, known as Prew to his friends. He is a man with a high personal integrity, who has no other choice in his life but the army. He has given up boxing because of the damage he did in the ring to another boxer. However, his individuality leads to a conflict with the system itself. He refuses to join the boxing squad and Captain Holmes warns him that "in the Army it's not the individual that counts". Holmes attempts to break his spirit. Prewitt becomes involved with a bargirl. When his friend Angelo Maggio is badly beaten in the Hickam Field Stockade by the sadistic Sgt. James R. "Fatso" Judson, Prewitt kills him with a knife, and is killed when he tries to return to his unit. Milt Warden, the highly competent Top Sergeant, has an affair with the wife of Captain Holmes, and cannot help Prewitt. Most of the story takes place before the Japanese surprise attack. With Norman Mailer's The Naked and the Dead (1948) the novel is among the best works depicting the American army in the Pacific during World War II.

With the money he earned from his bestseller, Jones purchased and furnished a house in Marshall, Illinois, and established a writers' colony with the assistance of Lowney Handy; she was also Jones's mistress and introduced him to her library of Eastern philosophy. When Norman Mailer visited Jones in 1953, they had a conversation about the ideas of Karma. "It's the only thing that makes sense," Jones argued for Mailer's surprise. After gaining financial independence, Jones was very generous to his fellow writers, and at one point he paid the poet Delmore Schwartz's hospital bills.

Mailer's attitude toward Jones became strained, Mary McCarthy called Jones "intelligent" and "uneducated," but William Styron remained his friend, observing that "there was a certain grandeur in Jones's vision of the soldier. . . . ." Ernest Hemingway wrote about Jones to their mutual publisher, Charles Scribner: "I hope he kills himself as soon as it does not damage his or your sales."

Jones was very sensitive to criticism about his work and worked for seven years before his second book, *Some Came Running* (1957), was published. Jones dedicated the novel to his younger sister, Mary Ann, who died of a brain tumour. It drew on his life in Illinois after the war and did not gain much critical acclaim. Frank MacShane described the novel in his biography about Jones "more like a nineteenth-century novel, infused with social consciousness and sympathy for the characters. The reader therefore does not know whether to take the story straight or to accept its basic absurdity..."

In 1974 Jones was offered a teaching position at Florida International University in Miami. At the end of the 1976 school year, the Jones moved to Southampton, New York. He died in Long Island, on May 9, 1977. James Ivory's film 'A Soldier's Daughter Never Cries' (1998), starring Kris Kristofferson, was largely based on the autobiographical novel by Kaylie Jones, the daughter of James Jones.

KINGSLEY AMIS

16.04.1922 – 22.10.1995

Sir Kingsley Williams Amis was an English novelist, poet and teacher and his literary work includes short stories, poetry, books of criticism, food and drinking writing, radio and television scripts and a number of novels in the genre of science and fiction, and mysteries. His poetry collections are known for his straightforward style and are often classified as anti-romanticism. Kingsley's most notable works include his first novel Lucky Jim, which became an exemplary novel of 1950's in Britain.

Kingsley Amis was born on 16 April 1922 in Clapham, a place in south London. His father, William Robert Amis was a mustard manufacturer's clerk. Kingsley received his primary education from the City of London School and enrolled into St. John's College, Oxford, in year 1941. After less than a year in 1942, he was admitted into army service, where he served in the Royal Corps of Signals during the Second World War. With the ending of the war in 1945, he returned to Oxford and resumed his studies and got a distinction in English. In 1946, Kingsley joined the Communist Party of Great Britain.

Kingsley was appointed as lecturer at the University of Wales Swansea in 1948, where he worked till the year 1961. It was then that he wrote his first novel Lucky Jim, which became the most praiseworthy novel of 1950's Britain. He was a visiting fellow researcher in creative writing at Princeton University in the United States and a visiting lecturer in other northeastern universities as well. After serving for thirteen long years at the University of Wales Swansea, he became a fellow of Peterhouse at Cambridge in 1961; though he regretted the decision very soon and resigned in 1963.

Kingsley's literary works is known for its wide variety and reach to every genre - novels, scripts, short stories, science and mystery. In his early career, he gained recognition as a comedy novelist though the multiplicity of his work removed this tag later and he became known as the master of every genre. Originally inclined to be a poet, Kingsley wrote poetries which draw heavily for their simple and accessible approach.

As a novelist, his first novel *Lucky Jim* may well be termed as his most famous work which was apparently a part of the Angry Young Men movement in Britain. He wrote novels that were a reflection of his own life and thoughts. Among his other popular works was *That Uncertain Feeling,* which came in 1955, and I like It Here, published in 1958. 'Take a girl like you' which was published in 1960, was his second best novel after *Lucky Jim* and gained him a huge popularity as an author.

After 1960, Kingsley embarked on writing about science and mystery fictions as well as the comedy ones. He later shifted from mystery to horror genre and wrote a successful book *The Green Man* in 1969. Before that he had written *The Anti-Death Leagues,* which was based upon imaginary incidents and characters. An atheist, Kingsley wrote poems and stories which showed his scornfulness towards God and religious beliefs. Meanwhile, he produced several essays and social criticism mainly for journalistic publication.

In the late 1960s, Amis became writing James Bond novels. In 1965, he wrote the James Bond Dossier and for the first time it was attributed to him, before that, he had been writing it under a pseudonym or a false name. In the same year, he wrote *The Book of Bond,* which was also known as *Every Man His Own 007.* Towards the end of his career, he turned as an Anthologist and wrote a number of poems and essays.

Kingsley Amis suffered from a mild stroke in 1995 which worsened his already ill health. After suffering for few months, he eventually died on 22 October 1995 at a hospital in London.

ALISTAIR MACLEAN

21.04.1922 – 02.02.1987

Alistair MacLean was born in Glasgow, the son of a minister. The family spoke the Scottish language, Gaelic, and English was MacLean's second language; at home he was not allowed to speak English. The family moved north to Daviot, near Inverness, and MacLean spent his early years in the Scottish Highlands. His father died of cerebral haemorrhage when Alistair was 14, and he returned to Glasgow with his mother Mary. MacLean's brother Lachlan, who was a medical student, died of cancer of the stomach.

After completing his Higher Leaving Certificate with passes in English, History, Latin, Mathematic and Science at Hillhead HighMacLean took up a post at the shipping office of F.C. Strick. At the age of eighteen in 1941, he joined the Royal Navy. During World War II he served as a torpedo man in Home, Mediterranean, and Eastern Fleets on the HMS Royalist. Much of the time he served on Russian convoy routes, and from these experiences he drew heavily for his novels about the sea. "He was a good chap to have around in a tight situation," recalled one of his shipmates. MacLean claimed that he was once captured by the Japanese and tortured, but his story has not been verified. However, in 1946 he returned home.

After the war, MacLean gained an English Honours degree at Glasgow University, and became a teacher at Gallowfleet Secondary School. During his spare time MacLean began writing short stories. In 1954 he entered a short story competition of the *Glasgow Herald* with the 'Dileas.' It won the first prize of £100. The depiction of the force of the sea was from a born storyteller: "The Dileas would totter up on a wave then, like she was falling over a cliff, smash down into the next trough with the crack of a four-inch gun, burying herself right to the gunwales. And at the same time you could hear the fierce clatter of her screw, clawing at the thin air. Why the Dileas never broke her back only God knows - or the ghost of Campbell of Ardrishaig."

With encouragement from the publishing company Collins, MacLean wrote his first novel, *H.M.S. Ulysses*. It was based on his experiences on a navy ship escorting merchant vessels in the Arctic Ocean and became a bestseller. *H.M.S. Ulysses* is regarded alongside Herman Wouk's *The Caine Mutiny* (1951) and Nicholas Monsarrat's *The Cruel Sea* (1951) as one of the classic novels of navy ships. It deals with a convoy in the North Atlantic battling during World War II with submarines and foul weather. The emotional power in the end of the story, when the doomed Ulysses turns against the heavy German cruiser, has not been surpassed in any other naval war novel.

From 1955 MacLean devoted himself entirely to writing, with great success. His next books, *Guns of Navarone* (1957) and *South by Java Head* (1957), were war stories. The *Guns of Navarone* (1957) depicted a five men sabotage team sent to destroy two giant guns at Navarone. The book was filmed in 1961 and won an Academy Award for special effects. The producer and screenwriter Carl Foreman bought the screen rights of *The Guns of Navarone* in 1958. He was fascinated by the author's "gift for keeping his audience enthralled by the pace and drive of his tale. The novel had six colorful major characters, providing an opportunity for casting as many international stars." Gregory Peck played Captain Mallory in the film and was criticized for being at times a trifle wooden - David Niven was Corporal Miller. The women Foreman wrote into the story were played by the Greek actress Irene Papas and the Italian Gia Scala. In its sequel, *Force 10 from Navarone* (1968), a mixed group attempt to blow up a bridge vital to the Nazis in Yugoslavia. The film version was not produced until 1977. Robert Shaw and Edward Fox played the Peck and Niven roles respectively. Force 10 from Navarone did not gain success similar to its predecessor.

MacLean's later books were not as well received as his earlier ones. *The Way to Dusty Death* (1973) was set in the world of racing cars, and *The Golden Gate* (1976) was a kidnapping story, in which the President of the United States and two Arab leaders are taken hostage in the middle of the Golden Gate Bridge.

MacLean had started his career as a short story writer, and a few years before his death he published The Lonely Sea, a collection of stories, in which he proved again his skill in describing the power of the sea. The book included his very first prize-winning achievement, a tale of an old seaman who takes an old fishing boat out in a storm in order to rescue his two sons. "And then a miracle happened. Just that, Mr MacLean - a miracle. It was the Sea of Galilee all over again. Mind you, the waves were as terrible as ever, but just for a moment the wind dropped away to a deathly hush - and suddenly, off to starboard, a thin, high-pitched wail came keening out of the darkness." MacLean died of heart failure in Munich on February 2, 1987.

He was buried in Celigny, Switzerland. MacLean left a number of story outlines, commissioned by an American film company, to be written by other authors. He was married twice, first to the German-born Gisela Heinrichsen, who worked at Mearnskirk Hospital; they had three sons. In 1972 MacLean married Marcelle Gorgeus, the daughter of French music-hall entertainers, Georgius Guibourg and Marcelle Irvun. The marriage ended in divorce in 1977. According to the divorce settlement, she was given £400,000 and the right to a full length screenplay, called The Golden Girl, which MacLean had completed.

NORMAN MAILER

31.01.1923 – 10.11.2007

Norman Kingsley Mailer, better known by his pen name Norman Mailer, was an American novelist, journalist, playwright, screen, writer, essayist and film director. The author is credited with the birth and evolution of the 'New Journalism', a term used for narrative nonfictions- in America. Mailer's first literary effort was a 250 pages long story called 'Invasion from Mars' that he wrote when he was just nine. His first bestselling novel came in 1948 entitled as *The Naked and the Dead* and the huge success of it was followed by other novels *The Deer Park* and *An American Dream.* In 1980, Norman authored a book *The Executioner's Song,* which gained him the Pulitzer Prize for fiction in the same year. Mailer was awarded the Pulitzer Prize twice and the National Book Award once for his literary efforts. The great bard also won the Medal for Distinguished Contribution to American Letters from the National Book Foundation in 2005.

Norman Mailer was born on 31 January 1923 in Long Branch, New Jersey in America to Isaac Barnett, an accountant and businessman and his wife Fanny Schneider, who worked in a trucking company. The family settled in Brooklyn, New York soon after his birth and visited Long Branch mainly for holidaying at his grandfather's place who owned a small hotel there. Mailer had a younger sister Barbara, who was born in 1927. As a child, Mailer took keen interest in writing and wrote a 250 pages long story called Invasion from Mars when he was just nine.

However, it was not until the Harvard University that he decided to take writing as a career. He graduated from Boy's High School and enrolled into the Harvard University in year 1939 and received his B.S degree in aeronautical engineering in 1943. While at Harvard, he became immensely fascinated with writing and published his first story. The Greatest Thing in the World, in 1941 winning the Story magazine's college contest. Upon completing his graduation, Mailer joined the U.S. Army and served in Philippines during the World War II. Though he was not involved into the combat operation there, his experience in the army prepared the ground work for his bestselling novel *The Naked and the Dead.*

Mailer left the Army in 1946 and published his first novel *The Naked and the Dead* in 1948, when he was just 25 years old. At that time, he was studying at the Sorbonne in Paris. The book, which had extracts from the events during his Military service in the war, became an instant success and was ranked among one of the best American wartime novels. Initially rejected by several publishers because of the obscenity of its language, the book remained on the New *York Times* bestseller list for more than 60 weeks and was ranked one of the "One hundred best novels in English language" by the Modern Library.

Barbary Shore, another novel he published in 1951, was a dramatic interpretation of the Cold War politics surrounding in Brooklyn. The book did not receive the similar response and was rejected as a "piece of banal and ungraceful story". In late 1940's, Mailer became associated with the Hollywood and began to work as a scriptwriter. After returning to New York City in 1951, he embarked on writing manuscript for his third novel *The Deer Park* which was based upon his own experience with corruption and immorality in Hollywood.

The manuscript was rejected several times before it could come into print after a long time.

Mailer wrote his fourth novel *An American Dream* in 1964. The book met with a mixed response and was highly praised by many eminent writers and critics and is still in print. In 1980, Norman Mailer authored a book *The Executioner's Song,* which gained him the Pulitzer Prize for fiction in the same year. For the next few years he continued to work upon *Ancient Evenings,* his novel of Egypt which also became a bestseller despite some negative reviews it received initially. *Harlot's Ghost,* Mailer's longest novel was published in 1991. His final novel, *The Castle in the Forest* was based upon Hitler's childhood and was his second best novel after *The Naked and the Dead.* It was awarded 'Bad Sex in Fiction' by the *Literary Review* magazine.In the mid 1950's, Mailer embarked on writing counter culture essays and gained reputation as an anti-establishment essayist.

He wrote an essay 'The White Negro: Superficial Reflections' on the Hipsters in which he examines the evils in American society putting the blame partly on the black community. The essay which was originally printed in *Dissent* in 1956 and then reprinted in *Advertisements for Myself* in 1959 was widely condemned for its blasphemous content. In 1955, he became one of the founders of *The Village Voice,* a newspaper, for which he wrote a column 'Quickly' for a short period. Aside from these, he wrote a number of book reviews and essays for *Esquire, The New York Review of Books* and *Dissent Magazine.* He also worked as a scriptwriter for a movie based on his novel *Tough Guys Don't Dance* in 1987. In 1968, Mailer gained 'George Polk Award' for his work in *Harper's Magazine.* Norman Mailer died of acute renal failure on 10 November 2007, at the age of 84 after undergoing a lung surgery. His body rests in a cemetery in New York.

MAHASWETA DEVI

Born in 1926

Mahasweta Devi is a reputed Indian writer who was born in the year 1926 into a middle class Bengali family at Dacca, which is located in present day Bangladesh. She received her education from the prestigious Shantiniketan set up by great Indian philosopher and thinker, Rabindranath Tagore, that went on to become a part of the Visva Bharti University later on. Mahasweta Devi graduated from the University of Calcutta (now Kolkata) and this was followed by an MA degree in English from the Visva Bharti University.

Since her entire family had shifted to India by now, Devi began teaching at the Bijoygarh College in 1964. In those times, this particular college was a forum operating for elite female students. This phase was also utilized by Mahasweta Devi to work as a journalist and a creative writer. Of late, Mahasweta Devi is known to have been studying the life history of rural tribal communities in the Indian state of West Bengal and also women and dalits.

Mahasweta Devi is a social activist who has wholly involved herself to work for the struggles of the tribal people in states like Bihar, Madhya Pradesh and Chhattisgarh. In the fiction themed on Bengal which Devi writes, she often narrates the brutal oppression faced by the tribal people at the hands of the powerful upper caste persons comprising landlords, money-lenders and government officials in this belt.

During the 2006 Frankfurt Book Fair when India happened to be the first country to have been invited to this fair for a second time, Mahasweta Devi made a very touching inaugural speech which moved many among the listeners to tears. Inspired by the famous Raj Kapoor song, she said: "This is truly the age where the Joota (shoe) is Japani (Japanese), Patloon (pants) is Englistani (British), the Topi (hat) is Roosi (Russian), but the Dil (heart) is always Hindustani (Indian)".

Mahasweta Devi's first work, *Jhansi Ki Rani,* was a fictional reconstruction of Laxmibai, the picture of woman ruler who died fighting the British army in the mid-nineteenth century. Several of her other early works such as *Amrita Sanchay* (1964) and *Andhanmalik* (1967) are also set during the British colonial period. The Naxalite movement of the late 1960's and early 1970's were also an important influence in her work. Devi, in a 1983 interview, points to this movement as the first major event that she felt "an urge and an obligation to document" (Bandyopadhyay, viii). This leftist militant movement, which started in the Naxalbari region of West Bengal, began as a rural revolt of landless workers and tribal people against landlords and moneylenders. In urban centres, this movement attracted participation from student groups. Devi's 'Hajaar Chaurasi Ki Maa' (Mother) is the story of a upper middle class woman whose world is forever changed when her son is killed for his Naxalite beliefs. This book has recently been made into a Hindi-language movie called *Hazaar Chaurasi ki Maa* a by director Govind Nihalani.

Another important theme in the works of Mahasweta Devi involves the position of tribal communities within India. She is a long-time champion for the political, social and economic advancement of these communities, whom she characterizes as "suffering spectators of the India that is travelling towards the twenty first century" (*Imaginary*

Maps, xi). These concerns can be seen in works such as *Aranyer Adhikar* (Rights of the Forest) and anthologies such as her *1979 Nairhite Megh* (Clouds in the Southwestern Sky). *Aranyer Adhikar*, which was published in 1977, is based on the life of Birsa Munda, a tribal freedom fighter. She has also donated the prize money from both the Jnanpath and Magsaysay awards to tribal communities and continues to use her work to further the position of these groups in India.

This activism is central to Devi's understanding of the role of a writer in society: "I think a creative writer should have a social conscience. I have a duty towards society. Yet I don't really why I do these things. The sense of duty is an obsession. I must remain accountable to myself."

Gayatri Chakravorty Spivak, who has translated two collections of Devi's stories including those in *Imaginary Maps* into English, suggests that this interplay of activism and literary writing in Devi's fiction can be of substantial interest to current academic discourse and practices. Spivak insists that Devi's work suggests a model in which activism and writing can reflect upon each other, providing a necessary vision of inter-nationality, and the possibility of constructing a new kind of responsibility for the cultural worker.

JAMES WRIGHT

13.12.1927 – 25.03.1980

James Arlington Wright, one of the most prolific American poets of the 20th century, was the proud recipient of the Pulitzer Prize. Wright made a debut in the literary world in the year 1956, with *The Green Wall*. The book not only earned him rave reviews, but also won him Yale Series of Younger Poets Award. Thereafter, there was no stopping for this talented poet. His second book, *Saint Judas* came soon after and earned him Ohiona Book Award. Later on in his life, Wright shed the conservational style and adopted the contemporary writing style. It was his book *The Branch Will Not Break*, which gave Wright's new mode its maximum expression. Apart from the prestigious awards, Wright also received a grant from the Rockefeller Foundation.

James Arlington Wright was born in Martins Ferry, Ohio, on December 13, 1927. While his father had a job in a glass factory, his mother worked in a laundry. In 1943, when Wright was still in high school, he suffered a nervous breakdown and missed a year of school. Graduating a year late, in 1946, he joined the army and was stationed in Japan, during the American occupation. After coming back from the army, he joined Kenyon College and graduated with honors in 1952. There, instead of studying vocational subjects, Wright focused his attention on English and Russian literature. During his graduation, he had published 20 journals, won Robert Frost Poetry Prize and was elected to Phi Beta Kappa. In 1953, he married Liberty Kardules in

Martins Ferry. Thereafter, he moved to Vienna, along with his wife, to study at the University of Vienna. For a year, Wright studied the works of Theodor Storm and Georg Trakl, on a Fulbright fellowship.

In 1954, James Wright enrolled himself at the University of Washington. Studying under Theodore Roethke, he earned a master's degree and went on to pursue a doctoral degree. In 1957, he made his debut with *The Green Wall* and was awarded with the Yale Series of Younger Poets Award. Around the same time, i.e. after the publication of *The Green Wall*, Wright was offered the position of a professor at the University of Minnesota. In 1959, he attained his doctorate, with a thesis on Charles Dickens. While his professional life was soaring high, his personal life turned sour. The marriage with Liberty Kardules ended in a disaster and the two separated in 1962.

Around the time of his separation, Wright made friends with Robert Bly, a poet, who was struggling to make a mark in the world. Together, both of them explored the boundaries of poetic language and worked on European and Latin American poets, like Georg Trakl and Cesar Vallejo. Soon, his second collection, 'Saint Judas', was published in the distinguished Wesleyan University Press. Three years later, in 1962, he was awarded with the Ohiona Book Award for *Saint Judas*. During these years, Wright had become an illustrious poet. His works featured in the major publications and journals, such as the *Sewannee Review*, the *New Yorker* and *New Orleans Poetry Review*.

Despite his achievements in the literary field, the University of Minnesota had doubts about Wright's qualification for becoming a tenured professor, resulting in his relocation to Macalester College. In 1963, his third book, previously titled *Amenities of Stone*, was released under the name *The Branch Shall Not Break*. The book proved to be one of the most influential volumes of the 1960s. Also It also market Wright's movement, away from the conservative trend and style, and towards the more experimental, free verse.

After his teaching experience at the Macalester College, Wright held a similar position in the Hunter College (1966). A year later, in 1967, he met Edith Ann Runk (Annie) and eventually, the two of them married and moved to New York. The two gelled very well and explored each other's positive qualities. Apart from supporting Wright's poetry, Annie also tamed down his drinking habit. Around this time, he published *Shall We Gather at the River*, a collection that, one may say, unified because it seemed like one long poem or notes for a long poem.

James Wright and Annie were always on the move. They would spend their summers in Paris and Italy, travelling from one hotel to another, just lazing around and writing poetry. In his last year, Wright and his wife travelled throughout Europe, until September 1979. He would often write back, about his new found life, to his friends in the US. In the autumn of 1979, when Wright and Annie reached USA, the former got hospitalized with a severe sore throat. He was diagnosed with cancer, which was neither treatable, nor could be operated upon. In 1980, his last book, *This Journey* was published.

On the 25th of March, 1980, James Wright left for the heavenly abode. His funeral was held at the same church Wright and Annie got married in – Riverside Church.

ELIE WIESEL

Born in 1928

Elie Wiesel is a Jewish Romanian-American writer, professor and the author of the bestselling book *Night* as well as many other books dealing with Judaism, the Holocaust, and the moral responsibility of the people to fight hatred, racism and genocide. A Holocaust survivor, Wiesel lost his parents in his early childhood and escaped to France where he studied literature, philosophy, and psychology at the Sorbonne. Wiesel emerged as a noted journalist and eventually settled in America. Catholic writer Francois Mauriac successfully persuaded Wiesel to write his experiences of the *Holocaust* which he did in his memoir *Night*. While his most of the works indirectly address the appalling Holocaust, his literary excellence is often overshadowed by his role of a Holocaust testimony. In his later life, Wiesel emerged as a political activist and humanitarian and was awarded the Nobel Peace Prize in 1986 for voicing his concern about the "global crisis of humanity".

Elie Wiesel was born on 30 September 1928 in the town of Sighet, Transylvania, now a part of Romania. His father Chlomo Wiesel was an orthodox Jew and had a grocery store while Sarah, his mother, was a daughter of a farmer. Growing up in a small village in Romania, Elie's world revolved around family, religious study, community and God. Chlomo instilled a strong sense of humanism in his son, encouraging him to learn modern Hebrew and to read literature, whereas his mother encouraged him to study Torah and Kabbalah. Elie grew up speaking Yiddish at home, and Hungarian, Romanian, and German outside.

After the liberation of the camps in April 1945, Wiesel spent a few years in a French orphanage where he was reunited with his older sisters, Hilda and Bea. Like many survivors, Wiesel could not find the words to describe his experiences and even after ten years of the war, Wiesel refused to write about or discuss his experiences during the Holocaust. In 1948, Elie Wiesel began to study literature, philosophy, and psychology at the Sorbonne in Paris. He gradually became involved in journalistic work with the French newspaper *L'arche*. He wrote for Israeli and French newspapers, including *Tsien* in Kamf. It was on the urging of Catholic writer Francois Mauriac, the 1952 Nobel Laureate in Literature, that Elie Wiesel wrote about his experiences in the death camps. The result was his internationally acclaimed memoir *And the World Remained Silent*, in Yiddish, and *La Nuit* or Night in French.

Elie Wiesel was awarded the Nobel Peace Prize in 1986 for speaking out against violence, repression, and racism. He has also been honoured with numerous prizes including The Congressional Gold Medal in 1985 and The International Center in New York's Award of Excellence. In 1996, Elie Wiesel was elected to the American Academy of Arts and Letters. Wiesel started the Elie Wiesel Foundation for Humanity and served as chairperson of the U.S. Holocaust Memorial Council from 1978 to 1986. On November 30, 2006 Wiesel received an honorary knighthood in London in recognition of his work towards raising Holocaust education in the United Kingdom. He is also the Founding President of the Paris-based Universal Academy of Cultures. Elie Wiesel has received over one-hundred honorary degrees from institutions of higher learning.

A. K. RAMANUJAN

1929 – 1993

Attipat Krishnaswami Ramanujan or A. K. Ramanujan, as he is known, was born in Mysore, India, in 1929. He was a transitional figure in the history of Indian English Literature, and also a trans-disciplinary scholar, working as a poet, translator, linguist, and folklorist. Although he wrote primarily in English, he was fluent in both Kannada and Tamil, the language of his family. Ramanujan received his BA and MA in English language and literature from the University of Mysore. He then spent some time teaching at several universities in South India before getting a graduate diploma in theoretical linguistics from Deccan University in Poona in 1958.

He went to the U.S. in 1959. In 1962, he became an assistant professor at the University of Chicago, where he was affiliated throughout the rest of his career. The following year, he went to Indiana University where he got a Ph.D. in linguistics in 1963. He taught at several U.S. universities, including Harvard, University of Wisconsin, University of Michigan, University of California at Berkeley, and Carlton College. At the University of Chicago, Ramanujan was instrumental in shaping the South Asian Studies Programme. He worked in the departments of South Asian Languages and Civilizations, Linguistics, and with the Committee on Social Thought. In 1976, the Government of India awarded him the honorific title "Padma Sri," and in 1983, he was given the MacArthur Prize Fellowship. Ramanujan breathed his last in Chicago on July 13, 1993.

Ramanujan was a major figure in shaping South Asian studies. According to him, the Indian way of thinking is "context-sensitive" as opposed to "context-free." Context-sensitive is, he suggests, the more appropriate term for what others have taken for an Indian tendency toward inconsistency and hypocrisy, as well as, perhaps tolerance and mimicry. Ramanujan cites Said's Orientalism here, suggesting a European source for these stereotypes created out of a necessity to essentialize and exoticize the Eastern world. These terms, he takes from linguistics, in which they refer to different kinds of grammatical rules.

In applying them to cultures or ways of thinking, Ramanujan relies primarily on a text-based analysis. He cautions that they are "overall tendencies." "Actual behaviour may be more complex, though the rules they think with are a crucial factor guiding the behaviour". Context-free thinking, which he attributes to Euro-American culture, gives rise to universal testaments of law, such as in the Judeo-Christian tradition and in the European philosophical tradition, e.g., Hegel. Context-sensitive thinking, on the other hand, gives rise to more complicated sets of standards such as the Laws of Manu, by which appropriateness depends on various factors, especially factors of identity and personhood, such as birth, occupation, life stage, karma, dharma, etc. Ramanujan stresses that this difference in philosophical outcome is not a symptom of irrationality, but a different kind of rationale.

Ramanujan's work in socio-linguistics also speaks to the critique of Sanskritic Indology. As shown in his 1964 essay with W. Bright, 'Sociolinguistic Variation and Language Change', Ramanujan opposes those who would conceive a monolithic standard grammar for Indian languages. Rather, he seeks to legitimize the vast variety of linguistic dialects. Specifically, here, Ramanujan and Bright compare a Brahmin

Tamil dialect with a non-Brahmin Tamil dialect. The Brahmin dialect, they found, was much more inflected with Sanskrit loan words and styles, whereas the non-Brahmin dialect tended to shift by innovation on existing phonologic and morphologic features rather than by foreign adoption. Ramanujan and Bright do not address the political and economic implication of this differential grammatical shift. However, their point, in 1964, was only to acknowledge and legitimize linguistic innovation as it occurs in various social groups in India.

Ramanujan wrote poetry almost entirely in English. The poet is known for his rather atavistic poetic arguments – arguments which disrupt common expectations. Ramanujan is not a poet of easy moral expectations. Where conventional morality collapses, poetry takes off. In Ramanujan's quirky universe, excellence in human affairs is more a product of one's compulsions or handicaps rather than one's innate genius. Reviewer Bruce King called Ramanujan one of the "Indo-Anglian harbingers of literary modernism". This description highlights several characteristics of Ramanujan's poetry, perhaps less common in other transcultural poetry. Characteristics of his modernist style include an almost jarring realism and hints at a kind of confessional style. Themes of hybridity and transculturation are also highlighted in his poetry.

SRI CHINMOY

27.08.1931 – 11.10.2007

Chinmoy Kumar Ghose was born in a village of East Bengal, 1931, to an affectionate and spiritually inclined family. Orphaned at age 12, he joined his siblings at the Sri Aurobindo Ashram, Pondicherry. Throughout the following 20 years in South India, he spent many hours a day in deep prayer and meditation, from which he received many profound experiences. These formative years bore a spring of creativity; though outwardly occupied in simple work, and developing as a notable sportsman, young Chinmoy's inner silence began to reveal prolific songs and poems.

Acting on a direction from his meditation, Sri Chinmoy moved to New York in 1964, to share his inner wealth with the Western world. He began with a small number of students, giving individual tuition, as well as public lectures, on what has become known as "The Path of the Heart." These teachings aim to remind the sincere seeker that truth, joy, and wisdom reside within; with a simple, pure and cheerful approach to life, alongside regular meditation on the heart, one can re-discover this inner birthright, and thus weave it into everyday life.

From his arrival in America in 1964 to his passing in 2007, at age 76, Sri Chinmoy travelled extensively, giving public musical performances, lectures, and meditations. He was warmly received around the globe, by such figures as Mikhael Gorbachev, Nelson Mandela, and Mother Teresa.

He held weekly meditations at the United Nations, from 1970 to 2007.

Sri Chinmoy Centres have now developed all over the world, offering free meditation courses, concerts and exhibitions, and hosting sporting events. Amongst these is the longest foot race in the world - 3,100 miles - staged annually in New York, and the World Harmony Run - a global torch relay. In the field of sport, as in life itself, Sri Chinmoy's motto is "self-transcendence" - the bettering of one's own achievements, and striving beyond one's perceived limitations. Though in his 70s, Sri Chinmoy is constantly seeking new goals and different outlets for his creativity, so as to inspire others to do the same. The youthful athlete has become a renowned weight-lifter, recently lifting 270 lbs using his wrist. From the piccolo to the pipe organ, he has offered concerts at the Royal Albert Hall, the Sydney Opera House, the Great Wall of China, and myriad locations in between. He wrote over 18,000 songs and published over 1,400 books of his writings, in the hope of being of service and inspiration to others.

V.S. NAIPAUL

Born in 1932

V.S. Naipaul is a noble laureate who won Nobel Prize in Literature in 2001. Though of Indian origin, V.S. Naipaul was born in Trinidad and is currently a British citizen.

V.S. Naipaul (Sir Vidiadhar Surajprasad Naipaul) was born on August 17, 1932, at Chaguanas, Trinidad and Tobago. His forefathers came as indentured labourers from India. Naipaul's upbringing familiarised him with every sort of deprivation, material and cultural. He got a scholarship to Oxford University and thus came to England. It was at Oxford that V.S. Naipaul discovered the writer in him.

V.S. Naipaul travelled extensively in India and Africa. At that time decolonisation was taking place and V.S. Naipaul observed from close quarters the resulting turmoil of emotions. These observations were reflected in his writings. V.S. Naipaul has written about slavery, revolution, guerrillas, corrupt politicians, the poor and the oppressed, interpreting the rages so deeply rooted in our societies.

V.S. Naipaul's fiction and especially his travel writing have been criticised for their allegedly unsympathetic portrayal of the Third World. But his supporters argue that he is actually an advocate for a more realistic development of the Third World. V.S. Naipaul's contempt for many aspects of liberal orthodoxy is uncompromising, but at the same time he has exhibited an open-mindedness toward some Third World leaders and cultures that isn't found in western writers.

V.S. Naipaul has discussed Islam in several of his books and he has been criticised for harping on negative aspects of Islam. V.S. Naipaul's support for Hindutva has also been controversial. He has been quoted describing the destruction of the Babri Mosque as a "creative passion", and the invasion of Babur in the 16th century as a "mortal wound."

V.S. Naipaul has won several awards and honours for his writings. In 1971, Naipaul won the Booker Prize for his book *In a Free State* and became the first person of Indian origin to do so. He won the Jerusalem Prize in 1983 and Nobel Prize for Literature in 2001.

MANOJ DAS

Born in 1934

Manoj Das was born in a coastal village of Orissa in 1934 and grew up amidst Nature's splendour. But he also experienced its fury when a cyclone devastated his area, followed by a famine and an epidemic that killed thousands of people. Added to that, his affluent house was twice plundered by dacoits while Manoj, aged six then, looked on with disbelief. Such ups and downs in life probably enriched his creative mind at its formative stage. And by the time he was in high school, he had already published many works in his mother tongue, Oriya.

He taught English in a college at Cuttack before he came over to Sri Aurobindo Ashram at Pondicherry in 1963, where he continues to be a professor at the Sri Aurobindo International Centre of Education. He started writing in English in the late 1950s and today he can probably be called the foremost bilingual writer in India. Why did he start writing in English? He said, "... At one stage, I felt inspired to write in English because I was haunted by the feeling that much of the Indian fiction in English that claimed to project the Indian life and situation was not doing justice to its claim. I, though born in a village just before Independence and hence living through the transition at an impressionable age, I could present through English, a chunk of genuine India".

He has received many awards including the Padma Shree, Sahitya Akademi Award and the Saraswati Samman.

Some years ago, he was given the annual BAPASI Award by the Booksellers and Publishers Association of South India.Does he feel at home in Pondicherry? He feels he is an Indian first, wherever he is. He has lived in Pondicherry for more than four decades. He loves its ambience and has great regard for its people.Manoj Das is a formidable influence on contemporary Oriya literature. But outside Orissa, he is better known as an Indo-Anglian writer. Which of the two aspects of his literary personality would he wish to be remembered for? "That does not depend on my choice," he said and continued, "I have a wide readership in Orissa. In English I have a trusted and serious readership, but numerically smaller. If the quality of my writing matters, both the streams of my contribution should prove lasting in their own rights."

Through his nearly 300 short stories, Manoj Das had brought about an awareness about the rural Indian life. He has been a crusader against the invasion of India's intellectual climate by decadent values. He has stressed the divinity and psychic splendour inherent in man. No wonder, he has among his admirers celebrities such as Graham Greene, Keating, Dr. K.R.Srinivasa Iyengar and so many academics in the Western world.

SHASHI DESHPANDE

Born in 1938

Shashi Deshpande is a well known name in the field of Indian literature. She was born in Dharwad in Karnataka as the daughter of the renowned Kannada dramatist as well as a great Sanskrit scholar, Sriranga. She pursued her education in Dharwad, Bombay and Bangalore.

Shashi Deshpande had a very sharp mind. She received degrees in Economics and Law. In fact, she was a gold medalist. After getting married, she shifted to Bombay (now Mumbai). During her stay in Mumbai, she decided to pursue a course in Journalism. So, she got herself enrolled in the Bharatiya Vidya Bhavan. Thereafter, she took up a job as a journalist in the magazine *Onlooker*. She worked there for a couple of months.

While working in the magazine, she began writing and the first short story that she wrote got published in 1970. Her short stories headed their way in popular magazines like *Femina, Eve's Weekly* etc. Her maiden collection of short stories was published under the title *Legacy* in the year 1978. Her first novel, *The Dark Holds No Terrors* was published in 1980.

She had written a novel titled *That Long Silence,* which brought her lot of praise and appreciation. In fact, for her fabulous work in this novel, she received the Sahitya Akademi Award and Nanjangud Thirumalamba award. She has been actively involved in writing books for children.

BAPSI SIDHWA

Born in 1938

Bapsi Sidhwa was born in Karachi – a city now in Pakistan. She has taught in several International Universities and presently resides in Houston, Texas. A vocal proponent of women's rights in South Asia, she has also infused her works with strong female characters. She is also the recipient of many awards, including the Sitara-e-Imtiaz, Pakistan's highest honor. Sidhwa's novel, *Cracking India,* (1991, U.S.; 1992, India; originally published as *Ice Candy Man,* 1988, England), is the basis for Deepa Mehta's 1998 film, 'Earth'. This story is set in Lahore in the time period directly before and during the partition of India in 1947 and is told from the point of view of a young Parsi Zoroastrian girl.

Bapsi Sidhwa began her writing career at the age of 26 after visiting the Karakoram mountain-area of Pakistan with her husband. She was touched by a tragic story of a young girl who had been brought to one of the area's tribes as a bride. After being there for a short time, the girl ran away from her husband's home. The tribals considered this a highly dishonourable act. Some of the men hunted her down and murdered her. Sidhwa first wrote a couple of short articles about the beauty of the Karakoram Mountains.

However, feeling compelled to tell the girl's story, she decided to make her first attempt at fiction writing and sat down to write a short story which turned into her first novel, *The Bride* (also in print as *The Pakistani Bride*). It is a work of fiction based on the events from the tribal girl's life. Her second novel, *Crow-eaters*, was a lively and humorous story about the Parsi community of Pakistan. Success didn't come to Bapsi Sidhwa without a lot of hard work. She wrote her first two novels in Pakistan where no one was publishing in English at the time.

So, after receiving many rejections, Sidhwa decided to self-publish and self-distribute *Crow-eaters*. In 1980, after receiving a copy of Sidhwa's self-published *Crow-eaters*, Britain's Jonathon Cape decided to publish it. The first two novels brought her recognition, it was her third novel, *Cracking India* (also published as Ice-Candy Man), that earned Bapsi Sidhwa international acclaim and acceptance as one of the most promising English novelists from South Asia, placing her among the likes of Kushwant Singh, Anita Desai, and R.K. Narayan. *Cracking India* won the Liberator Prize in Germany.

GIRISH KARNAD

Born in 1938

Born on May 19, 1938, in Matheran, Maharashtra, Girish Karnad has become one of India's brightest shining stars, earning international praise as a playwright, poet, actor, director, critic, and translator. As a young man studying at Karnataka University, Dharwar, where he earned a Bachelor of Arts degree in Mathematics and Statistics in 1958, Karnad dreamed of earning international literary fame, but he thought that he would do so by writing in English. Upon graduation, he went to England and studied at Oxford where he earned a Rhodes Scholarship and went on to receive a Master of Arts Degree in Philosophy, Politics and Economics. He would eventually achieve the international fame he had dreamed of, but not for his English poetry. Instead, Karnad would earn his reputation through decades of consistent literary output on his native soil.

His first play, *Yayati* (1961), was written neither in English nor in his mother tongue Konkani. Instead, it was composed in his adopted language Kannada. The play, which chronicled the adventures of mythical characters from the Mahabharata, was an instant success and was immediately translated and staged in several other Indian languages. His best loved play, however, would come three years later. By the time *Tughlaq,* a compelling allegory on the Nehruvian era, was performed by the National School of Drama, Karnad had established himself as one of the most promising playwrights in the country. He soon quit his post at the Oxford University Press, deciding to focus all of his energies on his writing.

For four decades, Karnad has continued to compose top-notch plays, often using history and mythology to tackle contemporary themes. He has also forayed into the jungle of cinema, working alternately as an actor, director, and screenwriter, and earning numerous awards along the way. At the age of sixty, however, Karnad is vowing to give up cinema for the stage. "I've had a good life," he says. "I have managed to do all I could wish for--even be a government servant! Now I feel whatever time I have left should be spent doing what I like best--writing plays."

Karnad's awards include the Mysore State Award for *Yayati* (1962), the Government of Mysore Rajyotsava Award (1970), Presidents Gold Medal for the Best Indian film for *Samskara* (1970), the Homi Bhabha Fellowship for creative work in folk theatre (1970-72), the Sangeet Natak Academy (National Academy of the Performing Arts) Award for playwriting (1972), the Kamaladevi Award of the Bharatiya Natya Sangh for the Best Indian play of the year for *Hayavadana* (1972), the National Award for Excellence in Direction for *Vamsha Vriksha* (shared with B.V. Karanth - 1972), the Mysore State Award for the Best Kannada film and the Best Direction for *Vamsha Vriksha* (1972), the Presidents Silver Medal for the Second Best Indian film for *Kaadu* (1974), the Padma Shree Award (1974), the National Award for the Best Kannada film for *Ondanondu Kaaladalli* (1978), the National Award for the Best Script for *Bhumika* (shared with Shyam Benegal and Satyadev Dubey - 1978), the Film Fare Award for the Best Script for *Godhuli* (shared with B.V. Karanth - 1978), the Best Bengal Film Journalists Association Award for the Best Actor in *Swami* (1978), the Karnataka Nataka Academy Award (1984), the Nandikar, Calcutta, Award for Playwriting (1989), the Golden Lotus for the Best Non-Feature Film for *Kanaka Purandara* (1989), the National Award for the Best Non-Feature Film on Social Issues for *The Lamp in the Niche* (1990), etc.

He also served as Director of the Film and Television Institute of India (1974-75), President of the Karnataka Nataka Academy (1976-78), Indian Co-Chairman for the Joint Media Committee of the Indo-U.S. Sub-Commission on Education and Culture (1984-93), Visiting Professor and Fulbright Scholar in Residence at the University of Chicago (1987-88), and Chairman of the Sangeet Natak Academy of Performing Arts (1988-93).

BHARATI MUKHERJEE

Born in 1940

Bharati Mukherjee was born on July 27, 1940, to an upper-middle class Hindu Brahmin family in Calcutta (now Kolkata), India. The second of three daughters of Sudhir Lal, a chemist, and Bina (Banerjee) Mukherjee, she lived with 40 or 50 relatives until the age of eight. Born into an extraordinarily close-knit and intelligent family, Mukherjee and her sisters were always given ample academic opportunities, and thus have all pursued academic endeavours in their careers and have had the opportunity to receive excellent schooling. In 1947, her father was given a job in England and he brought his family to live there until 1951, which gave Mukherjee an opportunity to develop and perfect her English language skills.

Mukherjee earned a B.A. with honors from the University of Calcutta in 1959. She and her family then moved to Baroda, India, where she studied for her Master's Degree in English and Ancient Indian Culture, which she acquired in 1961. Having planned to be a writer since childhood, Mukherjee went to the University of Iowa in 1961 to attend the prestigious Writer's Workshop. She planned to study there to earn her Master's of Fine Arts, then return to India to marry a bridegroom of her father's choosing in her class and caste.

Finally fed up with Canada, Mukherjee and her family moved to the United States in 1980, where she was sworn in as a permanent U.S. resident. Continuing to write, in

1986 she was awarded a National Endowment for the Arts grant. After holding several posts at various colleges and universities, she ultimately settled in 1989 at the University of California, Berkeley. Because of the distinctly different experiences she has had throughout life, she has been described as a writer who has lived through several phases of life.

She then led a life of exile as a post-colonial Indian in Canada. Finally, she shifted into a celebratory mode as an immigrant, then citizen, in the United States. She now fuses her several lives and backgrounds together with the intention of creating a "new immigrant" literature.

ANNE TYLER

Born in 1941

American novelist and short-story writer, whose keen ear for dialogue and life-like characters have won critical acclaim. Several of Tyler's novels have been set in Baltimore and focus on middle-class families, their secrets, ambitions, dreams, and crises. Among Tyler's best-known books is *The Accidental Tourist* (1985), which was made into a successful film, and the Pulitzer Prize winner for *Breathing Lessons* (1988).

"I mean you're given all these lessons for the unimportant things - piano-playing, typing. You're given years of lessons in how to do in normal life. Or marriage, either, come to think of it. Before you can drive a car you need a state-approved course of instruction, but driving a car is nothing, compared to living day in and day out with a husband and rising up a new human being." (from *Breathing Lessons*, 1988)

Anne Tyler was born in Minneapolis, Minnesota, but grew up in North Carolina, as the daughter of Lloyd Parry Tyler, an industrial chemist, and Phyllis Mahon Tyler, a social worker. Before settling in Raleigh, North Carolina, the family lived among various Quaker communities in the rural south. These years formed background for Tyler's Southern literary flavor, which is seen in the settings of her fiction. Also the writer Eudora Welty, who has depicted the Mississippi of her childhood, has influenced Tyler.

The Tylers moved several times in their search for an ideal place to raise their children. In 1948, when Anne was six, the Tyler family found the Celo Community, near Burnsville, in the mountains of North Carolina. The community operated on a shared labor basis. At Celo the Tylers lived in their own house, raised some stock, and used organic farming techniques. The children in the settlement received lessons in art, carpentry, and cooking. Anne attended also a small local public school at Harvard. According to a story, whenever the school's principal had to take a short leave to look after his cows, Anne was put in charge.

By the age of seven Anne had started to write stories. Most of these early writings concerned "lucky, lucky girls who got to go west in covered wagons." Her favourite book was *The Little House* by Virginia Lee Burton. Later she has said that the book showed her "how the world worked, how the years flowed by and people altered and nothing could ever stay the same." At the age of 19 Tyler graduated from Duke University, Durham, North Carolina, where she twice won the Anne Flexner Award for creative writing. Her first published short story, 'Laura,' appeared in Duke University's literary magazine, the Archive. She became a member of Phi Beta Kappa and did post-graduate work in Russian studies at Columbia University. Before settling in Baltimore, her home town for much of her adult life, Tyler was a bibliographer at Duke University, ordering books from the Soviet Union, and worked in the law library of McGill University. Tyler married in 1963 the Iranian-born child psychiatrist Taghi Modarressi; they had two daughters. Her husband died in 1997.

As a writer Tyler made her debut with *If Morning Ever Comes* (1964). It depicted a young man, Ben Joe Hawkes, who returns from Columbia to North Carolina and attempts to find his own way under family expectations. He knows that his father had lived alternately with his wife and mistress and his grandmother married his grandfather although she was in love with another man. Finally Ben must decide how to continue with his ex-girlfriend.

In 1967 Tyler became a full-time writer. She won in 1977 an award from the American Academy for *Earthly Possessions.* Her novel *Dinner at the Homesick Restaurant* (1982) explores tensions inside a family – the family is for Tyler the basic battlefield of all society. The events are seen from the perspective from each member in turn. Pearl Cody Tull's children have all their own view of her she is violently abusive, suspicious, or nurturing. Absentminded Ezra, the youngest son, runs the restaurant of the title, where Pearl's husband and her children gather for dinner after her funeral.

The *Accidental Tourist* won in 1986 National Book Critics Circle Award and was made into a film in 1988, directed by Lawrence Kasdan and starring William Hurt and Kathleen Turner. The protagonist is Macon Leary, who writes travel guides for travel-hating businessmen. After his son, Ethan is murdered in a fast-food joint and his wife Sarah leaves him, Macon spends his time in planes, addicted to routine. "He approved planes. When the weather was calm, you couldn't even tell you were moving. You could pretend you were sitting safe at home. The view from the window was always the same – air and more air – and the interior of one plane was practically interchangeable with the interior of any other." Macon's routines are shattered when he meets Muriel Pritchett, a dog trainer and her young son. Macon moves in with Muriel, but Sarah wants him back. As is many Tyler's novels, the characters are hesitant to flee their present lives. In this story Tyler also reassures that what ever happens, life goes on. *The Amateur Marriage* (2003), Tyler's sixteenth novel, shows on the other hand, that domestic conflicts have the tendency to continue several generations. Michael Anton and Pauline Barclay marry during the early World War II years. The dissolving of their marriage takes decades.

VIKAS SWARUP

Vikas Swarup was born in Allahabad in a family of lawyers. He did his schooling from Boys' High School & College, Allahabad, and pursued further studies at Allahabad University with subjects Psychology, History and Philosophy. He joined IFS in 1986. He is married to Aparna and they have two sons, Aditya and Varun.

He is presently, since August 2006, posted in Pretoria as India's Deputy High Commissioner to South Africa. His debut novel, *Q and A,* tells the story of how a penniless waiter in Mumbai becomes the biggest quiz show winner in history. Critically acclaimed in India and abroad, this international bestseller is being translated into 40 languages. It was shortlisted for the Best First Book by the Commonwealth Writers' Prize and won South Africa's Exclusive Books Boeke Prize 2006, as well as the Prix Grand Public at the 2007 Paris Book Fair.

A BBC radio play based on the book won the Gold Award for Best Drama at the Sony Radio Academy Awards 2008 and the IVCA Clarion Award 2008. Harper Collins brought out the audio book, read by Kerry Shale, which won the Audie for best fiction audio book of the year. The movie titled *Slumdog Millionnaire,* directed by Danny Boyle, was first released in the US to great critical acclaim. It won the People's Choice Award at the Toronto Film Festival and three awards (Best Film, Best Director and Most Promising Newcomer) at the British Independent Film Awards 2008. The National Board of Review picked Slumdog Millionnaire as the best film of 2008.

The movie swept five awards out of its six nominations at the Critics' Choice Awards, and all four nominations awarded at the Golden Globe Awards which includes best director, picture, screenplay & score, and seven BAFTA Awards. It received 10 Oscar nominations of which it won 8, including Best Picture and Best Director. From The NY Times' report: "Though it had no actors nominated for prizes, [it also] swept many awards other than those on the top line, including prizes for cinematography, sound mixing, score and film editing. Slumdog's eight Oscars was the largest total won by a single film since 'The Lord of the Rings: The Return of the King' won 11 in 2004." The film was released in the UK on 9th of January 2009 and in India on 23rd January.

Vikas Swarup's second novel *Six Suspects*, published by Transworld, was released on July 28, 2008 and is being translated into several languages. It has also been optioned for a film by the BBC and Starfield productions.

Swarup's short story 'A Great Event' has been published in 'The Children's Hours: Stories of Childhood', a bold and moving anthology of stories about childhood to support Save the Children and raise awareness for its fight to end violence against children.

Vikas Swarup has participated in the Oxford Literary Festival, the Turin International Book Fair, the Auckland Writers' Conference, the Sydney Writers' Festival, the Kitab Festival in New Delhi, the St. Malo International Book & Film Festival in France and the 'Words on Water' Literary Festival at the University of the Witwatersrand in Johannesburg.

SHOBHA DE

Born in 1947

Shobha De is an eminent Indian novelist, who is often known as India's Jackie Collins. She was born as Shobha Rajadhyaksha to a Saraswat Brahmin family of Maharashtra on the January 7, 1947. She completed her graduation from St. Xavier's College, Mumbai, and obtained degree in Psychology.

In the beginning of her career, she worked as a model and made a name for herself. Thereafter, she thought of changing her profession. Then, she pursued her career in Journalism. She brought out three magazines 'namely' *Stardust, Society,* and *Celebrity*. Presently, she is working as a freelance writer for a couple of newspapers and magazines.

These days, she is staying with her second husband Dilip De along with their children in one of the posh colonies of Mumbai. Most of her writings focus on different aspects of urban India. The erotic matter that she has written in the past has become the subject of controversy. She has also been actively involved in writing scripts for various TV soaps like Swabhimaan.

At present, she is working as a columnist and writes for a magazine *The Week*. In this periodical, she writes on varied issues concerning the society. She speaks her mind in her writings. She often expresses her dissatisfaction with respect to the behaviour exhibited by the present day generation. Many a times, she has been held responsible for accelerating the pace and bringing about a sexual revolution through her writings in the column "The Sexes" of the magazine *The Week*. She has also written a couple of erotic novels.

Shobha De is one of India's best-selling authors. She is the author of thirteen books all of which have topped bestseller lists in India, where she has revolutionised commercial women's fiction and redefined the mass-market bestseller. She is recognized as an important social commentator and an authority on popular culture. Outspoken and forthright, De chronicles today's India in her own inimitable style. *Bollywood Nights* is her first novel to be published in the UK. "Ms De shocks India, and much of its literary set like no other writer today", *New York Times*.

Shobha De is the author of the following books: *Socialite Evenings* (1989), *Starry Nights* (the original title of *Bollywood Nights* 1991), *Sisters* (1992), *Strange Obsession* (1992), *Sultry Days* (1994), *Snapshots* (1995), *Second Thoughts* (1996), *Surviving Men* (1997), and *Speedpost* (1999). She has also written the autobiographical *Selective Memory: Stories from My Life*.

SALMAN RUSHDIE

Born in 1947

Salman Rushdie is one of the most famous Indian origin authors. He is best known for the violent backlash his book *The Satanic Verses* (1988) provoked in the Muslim community. Iranian spiritual leader Ayatollah Khomeni issued a fatwa against Salman Rushdie, calling for his assassination, forcing Rushdie to go underground.

Salman Rushdie was born in Mumbai on June 19, 1947. When Rushdie was 17 his family migrated to Pakistan. Rushdie did his schooling from Cathedral and John Connon School in Mumbai, and Rugby School in Warwickshire. Salman Rushdie did his graduation in History from King's College, Cambridge. Following an advertising career with Ayer Barker, Salman Rushdie became a full-time writer.

Salman Rushdie began his writing career with *Grimus,* which was published in 1975. He gained literary fame with his second novel *Midnight's Children*. The book was awarded the 'Booker of Bookers' prize in 1993 after being selected as the best novel to be awarded the Booker Prize in its first 25 years. The novel narrates key events in the history of India through fiction. His third novel *Shame,* depicted the political turmoil in Pakistan with characters based on Zulfikar Ali Bhutto and General Muhammad Zia-ul-Haq. Salman Rushdie's latest novel was *Shalimar the Clown*. The novel was shortlisted for the 2005 Whitbread Novel Award.

Salman Rushdie has won many awards and honors. These include: Booker Prize for Fiction, James Tait Black

Memorial Prize (Fiction), Arts Council Writers' Award, "Booker of Bookers" or the best novel among the Booker Prize winners for Fiction, and Writers' Guild Award.

Rushdie's *The Satanic Verses* (1988) opens with the survival of two Indian men who fall out of the sky after their jumbo jet to England is blown up in midair by terrorists. These two characters then gain divine and demonic powers. Rushdie's habit of using the atrocities of history—especially involving religion—made *The Satanic Verses* a book of frightening recognition (describing events that have not yet occurred); another character in the novel is a writer sentenced to death by a religious leader.

The title of the novel refers to verses from the Koran, which were removed by later Islamic historians, describing a time when the Arab prophet (one with religious insight) Mohammed (the founder of Islam) briefly changed his belief in a single god and allowed mention to be made of three local goddesses. This was considered offensive and an insult to Islam by the Iranian leader Ayatollah Ruhollah Khomeini, who issued a fatwa, or religious order, calling for Rushdie's death. Rushdie went into hiding and received round-the-clock protection from British security guards. Rushdie's wife of thirteen months, author Marianne Wiggins, went into hiding with him when the death threat was announced. She soon emerged and announced that their marriage was over.

Khomeini's death threat extended not only to Rushdie himself, but to the publishers of *The Satanic Verses*, any bookseller who carried it, and any Muslim who publicly approved of its release. Several bookstores in England and America received bomb threats, and the novel was briefly removed from the shelves of America's largest bookselling chains. Two Islamic officials in London, England, were murdered for questioning the correctness of Rushdie's death sentence on a talk show. Many book-burnings were held throughout the world.

Rushdie himself, and his possible disguises in hiding, became the subject of many jokes. For example, during the 1990 Academy Awards presentation, which was seen worldwide by an estimated one billion viewers, comedian Billy Crystal joked that "the lovely young woman" who usually hands Oscar statuettes to their recipients "is, of course, Salman Rushdie."

In 1999 Rushdie published *The Ground Beneath Her Feet,* the story of a famous singer lost during an earthquake. Rushdie described it as "a novel of our age" in an interview with CNN's Jonathan Mann. In April 2000 Rushdie created a sensation by visiting India, his first visit to his birthplace since he was four years old. In November 2001 Rushdie told the *Manchester Guardian* that most Muslims' view of Islam is "jumbled" and "half-examined." He criticized Muslims for blaming "outsiders" for the world's problems and said that they needed to accept the changes in the modern world to truly achieve freedom.

VIKRAM SETH

Born in 1952

Vikram Seth was born on June 20, 1952 at Calcutta (now Kolkata). His father, Prem, was an employee of the Bata India Limited shoe company who migrated to post-Partition India from West Punjab in Pakistan. Vikram Seth's childhood was spent in the town of Batanagar near Calcutta, Patna near Danapur, and London. His mother Leila Seth was the first woman judge of the Delhi High Court as well as the first woman to become Chief Justice of a state High Court; she was the Chief Justice of Shimla High Court.

Vikram Seth did his schooling from the Doon School in Dehradun. He took his undergraduate degree in philosophy, politics and economics from Oxford University. He was enrolled in postgraduate economics courses at Stanford University and was also attached to Nanjing University for his intended doctoral dissertation on Chinese population planning.

Vikram Seth's first novel, *The Golden Gate* (1986), describes the experiences of a group of friends living in California. His other novel, *A Suitable Boy* (1993) is an acclaimed epic of Indian life. The novel won the WH Smith Literary Award and the Commonwealth Writers Prize (Overall Winner, Best Book). Set in India in the early 1950s, it is the story of a young girl, Lata, and her search for a husband. *An Equal Music* (1999), is the story of a violinist haunted by the memory of a former lover.

Vikram Seth has also written a travelogue *From Heaven Lake: Travels through Sinkiang and Tibet* (1983). The book is an account of a journey through Tibet, China and Nepal that won the Thomas Cook Travel Book Award. He also wrote a Libretto, *Arion and the Dolphin* (1994), which was performed at the English National Opera in June 1994, with music by Alec Roth. Vikram Seth is also an accomplished poet. His works in poetry include *Mappings* (1980), *The Humble Administrator's Garden* (1985), which was a winner of the Commonwealth Poetry Prize (Asia), and *All You Who Sleep Tonight* (1990). Vikram Seth has written a story book for children *Beastly Tales from Here and There* (1992), which consists of ten stories about animals told in verse.

After the success of *The Golden Gate,* Seth took up residence in his parents' house back in Delhi to work on his second novel, *A Suitable Boy* (1993). Though initially conceived as a short piece detailing the domestic drama of an Indian mother's search for an appropriate husband for her marriageable Indian daughter against the background of the formative years of India after Independence, the novel grew and Seth was to labour over it for almost a decade. The 1349-page novel is a four-family saga set in post-Independence, post-Partition India, and alternatively satirically and earnestly examines issues of national politics in the period leading up to the first post-Independence national election of 1952, inter-sectarian animosity, land reform and the eclipse of the feudal princes and landlords, academic affairs, inter- and intra-family relations and a range of further issues of importance to the characters. The Indian journalist and novelist Kushwant Singh has said of the novel that, "I lived through that period and I couldn't find a flaw. It really is an authentic picture of Nehru's India." The novel was, despite its formidable length, a bestseller, and propelled Seth into the public spotlight and assured his reputation. English critics greeted *A Suitable Boy* with almost universal enthusiasm (notwithstanding its somewhat controversial passing-over for the Booker Prize shortlist), though it received mixed reviews from some American critics.

His latest, *Two Lives,* is a non-fiction family memoir written at the suggestion of his mother, and published in October, 2005. It focuses on the lives of his great uncle (Shanti Behari Seth) and German-Jewish great aunt (Henny Caro) who met in Berlin in the early 1930s while Shanti was a student there and with whom Seth stayed extensively on going to England at the age of 17 for school at Tonbridge and then to attend Oxford. As with *From Heaven Lake, Two Lives* contains much autobiography and this is a considerable part of its appeal.

AMITAV GHOSH

Born in 1956

India-born Amitav Ghosh is a world renowned novelist and author. In his writing, Amitav Ghosh demonstrates the mixture and interstitial nature of cultures, as expressed through language. Like many subaltern authors, Amitav Ghosh endeavours to recuperate the silenced voices of those not represented in the historical record. Amitav Ghosh has held academic positions at a number of universities, including the Delhi University and the Columbia University.

Amitav Ghosh has received numerous awards for his works. Some of these awards are Prix Medicis Etranger for *The Circle of Reason* (1986), the Sahitya Akademi Award for *The Shadow Lines* (1988), the Arthur C. Clarke Prize for science fiction for *The Calcutta Chromosome* (1996), the Pushcart Prize for his essay, *The March of the Novel through History: My Father's Bookcase* and the Grand Prize for Fiction at the Frankfurt International e-Book Awards for *The Glass Palace*.

Ghosh has also written three works of non-fiction. They are *Countdown* (on India's nuclear policy) *The Imam and the Indian* (a collection of essays on different themes like fundamentalism, history of the novel, Egyptian culture and literature) and Dancing in Cambodia.

Amitav Ghosh was born in Calcutta (now Kolkata). His father was in the Indian army. It was mainly because of this reason that Amitav Ghosh got the chance to visit a number of countries including Sri Lanka, Iran and Bangladesh. Amitav Ghosh did schooling from the Doon School, Dehradun. He completed his graduation from St. Stephens College, Delhi University. After leaving St. Stephen's with a B.A. in History in 1976, he obtained an M.A. in Sociology from Delhi University in 1978. He went to St. Edmund Hall, Oxford, to pursue postgraduate work and in 1979 obtained a diploma in social anthropology. He also spent some time at Tunis where he learnt Arabic. Amitav Ghosh was awarded his Oxford D. Phil. in Social Anthropology for his thesis on "Kinship in Relation to the Economic and Social Organization of an Egyptian Village Community" in 1981.

Amitav Ghosh lives in New York with his wife, Deborah Baker, the author of *In Extremis: The Life of Laura Riding* (1993) and a senior editor at Little Brown and Co., and his children Leela and Nayan.

Amitav Ghosh's writings deal in the epic themes of travel and diaspora, history and memory, political struggle and communal violence, love and loss, while all the time crossing the generic boundaries between anthropology and art work. Both his fictional and non-fictional narratives tend to be transnational in sweep, moving restlessly across countries, continents and oceans. Formidably learned and meticulously researched, there is something equally epic about the scale of scholarship that sits behind each of his books. However, Ghosh never loses sight of the intimate human dimension of things. It is no coincidence that his writing ritually returns to Calcutta (the author's birth place), and, for all its global ambition, is thickly accented by the registers and referents of Bengali and South Asian culture.

Ghosh's first novel is typical in this sense. At the centre of *The Circle of Reason* (1986) is Alu, an eight-year-old

Bengali boy with a huge head, "curiously uneven, bulging all over with knots and bumps". These bodily deformities, along with the series of coincidences and connections that emerges between Alu's personal life and the political world around him, have led to obvious comparisons with Rushdie's Booker of Bookers, *Midnight's Children*. However, this is in some ways unfortunate as the novel has its own integrity and ambition, from its philosophical exploration of reason to its peripatetic wanderings across South Asia, North Africa and the Middle East.

Ghosh's beautifully written second novel, *The Shadow Lines* (1988), is also reminiscent of Rushdie in terms of its formal experimentations with geography and chronology. However, unlike Rushdie, it is written in an understated, condensed prose that comes close to poetry. The novel deals with the invention of the past and the arbitrariness of partition as it moves between India and the UK, Calcutta and London, the Second World War and present. The title is an allusion to Joseph Conrad's novella, *The Shadow Line*, and while its precise relationship to Conrad's text is oblique and shadowy, both share a preoccupation with the threshold between East and West, and with the ghostly hauntings of imperial memory. More generally, Ghosh's second novel draws inspiration from diverse modern European and Indian texts from Proust to Tagore, Ford Madox Ford to Satyajit Ray.

GITA SAHGAL

Born in 1956/1957

Gita Sahgal, born 1956/1957 in India, is a writer and journalist on issues of feminism, fundamentalism, and racism, a director of prize-winning documentary films, and a women's rights and human rights activist.

She has been a co-founder and active member of women's organizations. She has also been head of Amnesty International's Gender Unit, and one of Amnesty's leading voices against oppression of women, in particular by religious fundamentalists. In February 2010 she was suspended by Amnesty as head of its Gender Unit after she was quoted by *The Sunday Times* in an article about Amnesty, criticizing Amnesty for its high-profile associations with Moazzam Begg, the director of a campaign group called Cageprisoners, whom she referred to as "Britain's most famous supporter of the Taliban". Amnesty responded that she was not suspended "for raising these issues internally." Among those who spoke up in her support was Salman Rushdie.

In April 2010, Amnesty said that due to irreconcilable differences of view Sahgal would leave Amnesty on 9 April.

Sahgal is originally from India, and currently lives in England. She is the daughter of novelist Nayantara Sahgal. She is also the great-niece of former Indian Prime Minister Jawaharlal Nehru, and the granddaughter of his sister Vijayalakshmi Pandit. Schooled first in India, she then graduated from London's School of Oriental and African

Studies. When Sahgal returned to India in 1977, she joined the civil rights movement. She moved back to England in 1983. Born and raised in a Hindu background, she currently describes herself as an atheist.

She co-founded in 1979 and has been an active member of Southall Black Sisters. It is a non-profit organisation based in Southall, West London, that has worked against domestic violence, racism (often that of some white feminists), sexism (often that of some Black and Asian anti-racist campaigners), and bigotry.

She also co-founded in 1989 and has actively participated with Women against Fundamentalism. It was formed to challenge the rise of fundamentalism in all religions. One of its positions has been that as a Christian country with an established church and blasphemy laws that only protect Christianity, England encourages the growth of sectarianism by excluding immigrants, leading them to gravitate towards religious fundamentalism. In her early years in Delhi, India, Sahgal was part of a feminist network that fought against rape and dowry laws.

Commenting on the use of rape in wars, Sahgal said in 2004 that it is a mistake to think such assaults are primarily about "spoils of war" or sexual gratification. She said rape is often used in ethnic conflicts as a way for attackers to perpetuate social control and redraw ethnic boundaries. "Women are seen as the reproducers and careers of the community," she said.

NAMITA GOKHALE

Born in 1956

The writer Namita Gokhale was born in Lucknow, India, in 1956 and spent her childhood between New Delhi and Nainital, in the foothills of the Himalayas. A Kumaoni by birth she was married to Rajiv Gokhale when she was eighteen. Gokhale dropped out of college after a conflict over the bias against Indian literatures in the curriculum. She then published the enormously successful film magazine "Super" from Bombay in the late seventies.

Gokhale has written five novels and two works of nonfiction, all in English. Her first novel, *Paro: Dreams of Passion*, 1984, a satire upon the Mumbai and Delhi elite caused an uproar due to its candid sexual humour. *Gods, Graves and Grandmother* – an ironic fable about street life in Delhi was adapted into a musical play. Gokhale was diagnosed with cancer when she was just thirty-five and her husband died a few years later. The experience of illness and loss has informed her later books, *A Himalayan Love Story, The Book of Shadows* and *Shakuntala, the Play of Memory*. Gokhale has written two books of non-fiction, *Mountain Echoes* which deals with the Kumaoni way life through the eyes of four highly talented and individualistic women. *The Book of Shiva* is an introduction to Shaivite philosophy and mythology. She had retold the Indian epic, The Mahabharata, in an illustrated version for the young and first time readers. Her most recent publication *In Search of Sita – Revisiting Mythology*, co-edited with Dr. Malashri Lal, presents fresh interpretations of this enigmatic goddess and her indelible impact on the lives of Indian women.

Publishing is Gokhale's other love. The Namita Gokhale editions, a signature imprint published in association with Roli Books, introduced some notable titles including Rashna Imhasly Gandhy's *The Psychology of Love* and Neelima Dalmia Adhar's biography of her father, R K Dalmia. She has conducted two memorable writers' retreats in Landour, with Roli Books, for the Namita Gokhale editions. Gokhale is passionately committed to showcasing and translating the best of Indian writing and engaging the vibrant Bhasha languages of the Indian sub-continent in a creative dialogue with each other and the rest of the world. She is one of the founder directors of Yatra Books which co-publishes with Penguin Books in Hindi, Marathi, Urdu and other Indian languages including English in a ground-breaking series.

Namita Gokhale conceptualised the famous International Festival of Indian Literature, Neemrana 2002, and also The Africa-Asia Literary Conference, 2006. She has worked on groundbreaking seminars on Translating Bharat, and Textile Narratives with the literary consultancy, Siyahi. She is a founder-director of the Jaipur Literature Festival along with the author, William Dalrymple.

MANIL SURI

Born in 1959

Manil Suri was born in July, 1959 in Mumbai. He spent several years of his life acquiring degrees in mathematics, B.Sc. (1979), University of Bombay; M.S. (1980) and Ph.D. (1983), Carnegie-Mellon University, followed by several years climbing the academic ladder as a mathematics professor at the University of Maryland, Baltimore County as assistant (1983-89), associate (1989-94), full professor (1994-present).

In 1995, he did have his first story, "The Tyranny of Vegetables," published. Unfortunately, it was in a Bulgarian-language journal and he was only able to identify it by an author photograph next to the piece. He thinks the name of the journal is *Orpheus*, but as he is unable to read the title of the complimentary copy that came from Bulgaria, he cannot be sure.

He started *The Death of Vishnu* as a short story in 1995. It was inspired by the death of an actual man named Vishnu who had lived (and died) on the steps of the Bombay apartment building in which he grew up. By 1997, it had grown to three chapters, and he took it to a workshop at the Fine Arts Work Center in Provincetown, Massachusetts, led by Michael Cunningham. Cunningham began his critique with the exhortation to "keep writing this at any cost" and ended it with "you must do whatever is necessary to finish this." That's when Suri realized that perhaps the time for dabbling had come to an end, perhaps he had stumbled onto the start of something more serious. Three years later, an excerpt, "The Seven Circles" appeared in *The New Yorker*, bringing in his first non-Bulgarian audience.

In addition to Michael Cunningham, Suri has taken writing workshops with two other wonderful teachers: authors Jane Bradley and Vikram Chandra. He has been a fellow at the Virginia Center for the Creative Arts and the MacDowell Colony, and was the winner of the 1998 Jenny McKean Moore Residency Fellowship awarded biannually by George Washington University.

VIKRAM CHANDRA

Born in 1961

Vikram Chandra was born in New Delhi in 1961. His father, Navin Chandra, is a retired executive. His mother, Kamna Chandra, has written several Hindi films stories and plays; her most notable works include the films *Prem Rog* and *1942: A Love Story.* One of his sisters, Tanuja Chandra, is a filmmaker and screenwriter who has directed several films, including *Sur* and *Sangharsh.* His other sister, Anupama Chopra, is a film critic and consulting editor for India's NDTV.

Chandra received his high school education at Mayo College in Ajmer, Rajasthan, and attended St. Xavier's College in Mumbai. As an undergraduate student, he transferred to the United States. He graduated from Pomona College in Claremont, California, with a *magna cum laude* B.A. in English (concentration in Creative Writing). Chandra then attended, film school at Columbia University in New York, leaving halfway through to begin work on his first novel. He received his M.A. from The Writing Seminars at Johns Hopkins in 1987.

Red Earth and Pouring Rain, Chandra's first novel, was inspired by the autobiography of James Skinner, a legendary nineteenth century Anglo-Indian soldier. The novel was written over several years at the writing programmes at Johns Hopkins University and the University of Houston. It was published in 1995 by Penguin Books in India; by Faber and Faber in the UK; and by Little, Brown in the United States. *Red Earth and Pouring Rain* received outstanding critical acclaim, and it won both the Commonwealth Writers Prize for Best First Book and the David Higham Prize for Fiction. The novel is named after a poem from the Kuruntokai, an anthology of Classical Tamil love poems.

Love and Longing in Bombay, a collection of short stories, was published in 1997 by the same publishers as *Red Earth and Pouring Rain.* This collection of stories won the Commonwealth Writers Prize for Best Book (Eurasia region), was short-listed for the Guardian Fiction Prize, and was well received by international press and media.

In 2000, Vikram served as co-writer, with Suketu Mehta, for 'Mission Kashmir', a Bollywood movie directed by his brother-in-law, the award-winning director Vidhu Vinod Chopra, and starring Hrithik Roshan.

Sacred Games, Vikram Chandra's most recent novel, was published in 2006. Set in a sprawling Mumbai, it features Sartaj Singh, a policeman who first appeared in *Love and Longing in Bombay.* Over 900 pages long, *Sacred Games* was one of the year's most anticipated new novels and was the subject of a bidding war amongst the leading publishers in India, the UK, and the US.

ANITA RAU BADAMI

Born in 1961

Anita Rau Badami was born in 1961, in the town of Rourkela in Orissa, India. Her father, a mechanical engineer who designed trains, was transferred every two or three years, so that she had a mobile childhood. She grew up in a household where English was the primary language spoken and attended Catholic schools in India, because, as she explains, until around twenty years ago, these were the good schools in India.

At age 18, Anita Rau Badami borrowed money from her father to buy novels at a book fair in Chennai, India. To pay him back she took her first writing assignment, an article in a local newspaper, and earned 75 rupees. She holds degrees in Communication Media, English Literature, and Journalism from universities in Bombay and Madras. Badami began her career as a freelance writer in India with regular features in *The Hindu, The Deccan Herald,* and *Indian Express.*

She worked as a copywriter for advertising agencies in Bombay, Bangalore and Madras, and wrote stories for children's magazines. She married in 1984, had a son in 1987, and moved to Calgary in 1991. In 1995, she graduated from the University of Calgary where she received an M.A. degree in English. She submitted her first work to Penguin Books. Penguin published her work, and soon Badami was touring North America, reading from her best-selling debut novel *Tamarind Men.*

Several of her short stories appeared in Canadian literary journals such as *The Malahat Review, Event, Toronto Review of*

Contemporary Fiction, among others. *The Hero's Walk* was the winner of the Marian Engel Award for excellence in fiction for a body of work; a finalist in the 2000 Kiriyama Pacific Rim Prize for fiction; and on the longlist for the 2002 Orange Prize for Fiction.

The *Hero's Walk* was nominated for the 2002 International IMPAC Dublin Literary Award. The Hero's Walk also won the Commonwealth Best Book Prize in the Canada/ Caribbean region, as well as the Washington Post Best Book of 2001. Ms. Badami has taught writing at University of British Columbia.

Since moving to Montreal when her husband, Madhav, got a job teaching at McGill University, she has been working quietly on her third novel. She then received a call from Concordia offering her the position.

It was in Vancouver that she began working on her third novel, *Can You Hear the Night Bird Sing*. She has been contacted by her publishers in India and England to republish her children's stories, and she has had an idea for book number four. The working title is *The Guest.*

ARUNDHATI ROY

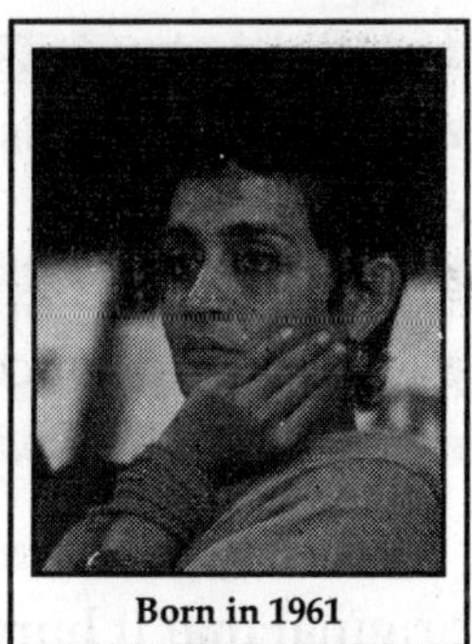
Born in 1961

Arundhati Roy was born on November 24, 1961 in Assam. Her mother was a Keralite Christian and her father was a Bengali Hindu. Their marriage was not successful and Arundhati Roy spent her childhood years in Aymanam, Kerala, with her mother. Arundhati's mother, who was a prominent social activist, founded an independent school and taught her daughter informally.

At the age of sixteen Arundhati left home, and eventually enrolled at the Delhi School of Architecture. There she met her first husband, Gerard Da Cunha, a fellow architecture student. Their marriage lasted four years. Both of them did not have great love for architecture, so they quit their profession and went off to Goa. They used to make cake and sell it on the beach to make a living. This continued for seven months after which Arundhati returned back to Delhi.

She took a job at the National Institute of Urban Affairs, rented a barsati near the dargah at Nizamuddin and hired a bicycle. One day film director Pradeep Krishen saw her cycling down a street and offered her a small role of tribal girl in the film "Massey Saab". Arundhati Roy accepted the role after initial reservations. Later on she married Pradeep Krishen. Meanwhile, Arundhati got a scholarship to go to Italy for eight months to study the restoration of monuments.

After returning from Italy Arundhati Roy linked with her husband to plan a 26-episode television serial for

Doordarshan called the Banyan Tree. The serial was later scrapped. She wrote screenplays for a couple of TV films - "In Which Annie Gives It Those Ones" and "Electric Moon". Arundhati Roy also wrote screenplay for Shekhar Kapur's controversial film 'Bandit Queen'. The controversy escalated into a court case, after which Arundhati Roy retired to private life to concentrate on her writings, which eventually resulted in *The God of Small Things.*

The God of Small Things heralds a voice so powerful and original that it burns itself into the reader's memory.

Sweet and heartbreaking, ribald and profound, this is a novel to set beside those of Salman Rushdie and Gabriel Garcia Marquez.

After winning the Booker Prize for *The God of Small Things,* Arundhati Roy has concentrated her writings on political issues. She has written on varied topics such as Narmada Dam project, India's nuclear weapons and American power giant Enron's activities in India. Arundhati Roy strongly associated with anti-globalization movement and is a staunch critic of neo-imperialism. She won the Booker Prize in 1997 for her first novel *The God of Small Things;* Awarded Sydney Peace Prize in 2004.

The twins at the centre of the novel, brother Estha and sister Rahel, are seven in December, 1969, and 31 in May, 1994, when the novel opens. Alternating between the two time periods, the narrative explores the impact of the tragic drowning of Sophie Mol, a nine-year-old cousin visiting India from London. Her death in 1969 was part of a complex series of events that destroyed the extended family and caused the formerly inseparable twins to be parted for over twenty-four years.

Following an unusual structure, Roy paints the broad strokes of the whole story in the first chapter. She then continues to circle around and around the central events, accumulating details and finally plunging into her narrative core at the end. This method is reflected in two striking images: of "a funnel of mosquitoes, like an inverted dunce cap" whining over people's heads, and especially the image of a group of bats that "coalesced and blackened" over the "History House" where key events take place, then suddenly plummet down through the "History-hole" in the roof. With its non-linear gathering, repetitions, and deferral of its most painful and ecstatic moments, Roy's intimate narrative reflects the logic of human memory sifting through the past to assess the damaged state of the present. Arundhati Roy is a famous Indian novelist and social activist.

Arundhati Roy was trained as an architect and is also an award-winning screenwriter. Like her twin protagonists, she was raised near her grandmother's pickle factory in Kerala, India. She now resides in New Delhi.

AMIT CHAUDHURI

Born in 1962

Amit Chaudhuri was born in Calcutta (now Kolkata) and grew up in Bombay (now Mumbai). He graduated from University College, London, and was a research student at Balliol College, Oxford. He was later Creative Arts Fellow at Wolfson College, Oxford, and received the Harper Wood Studentship for English Literature and Poetry from St John's College, Cambridge. He has contributed fiction, poetry and reviews to numerous publications including *The Guardian*, the *London Review of Books*, the *Times Literary Supplement*, the *New Yorker* and *Granta magazine*.

His first book, *A Strange and Sublime Address* (1991), a novella and a number of short stories, won the Betty Trask Prize, the Commonwealth Writers Prize (Eurasia Region, Best First Book) and was shortlisted for the Guardian Fiction Prize. His second novel, *Afternoon Raag* (1993), won both the Southern Arts Literature Prize and the Encore Award (for best second novel of the year). The novel adopts the metaphor of Indian classical music, the raag, to evoke the complex emotions displayed by the narrator, a young Indian student at Oxford. It was followed by *Freedom Song* (1998), set in Calcutta during the winter of 1992-93 against a backdrop of growing political tension between Hindus and Muslims. The US edition of *Freedom Song* won the Los Angeles Times Book Prize (Fiction) in 2000. *A New World* (2000) is the story of Jayojit Chatterjee, a divorced writer living in America, and the visit he makes with his son Vikram to his elderly parents' home in Calcutta.

His latest book, *Real Time* (2002), includes a number of short stories set in Bombay and Calcutta, some of which have been published in the *London Review of Books*, the *Times Literary Supplement* and the *New Yorker*, as well as *'E-minor'*, a memoir written in verse. *D. H. Lawrence and 'Difference': Postcoloniality and the Poetry of the Present,* exploring Lawrence's position as a 'foreigner' in the English canon, was published in 2003.

Amit Chaudhuri lives in Calcutta with his wife and daughter. He is editor of The Picador Book of Modern Indian Literature, published in 2001. His most recent book is *St. Cyril Road and Other Poems* (2005).

VIJAY SINGH

Born in 1963

Vijay Singh is an Indian novelist, screenplay-writer and film-maker living in Paris. A graduate in History from St Stephen's College, Delhi, with a postgraduate degree from Jawaharlal Nehru University, New Delhi, he moved to Paris for doctoral work at the Ecole des Hautes Etudes en Sciences Sociales. This move-over was precipitated principally by his passion for French literature and surrealism, particularly after a chance encounter with André Breton's *Manifestoes of Surrealism.*

While still a student in Paris, he started contributing articles to the French *Oress* in the early eighties. This was the beginning of his career as a journalist. He has written extensively for several leading French and international newspapers such as *Le Monde, Le Monde Diplomatique, Libération* and *The Guardian,* covering some of the most turbulent events of that epoch – Operation Blue Star, the Bhopal Gas tragedy, Indira Gandhi's assassination and its gruesome aftermath...

In 1984, a leading French publisher asked him to write a book on India. Vijay Singh decided to undertake a long and hazardous journey down the holy river Ganges, from its source in the snow-bound Himalayas to the Bay of Bengal. With this "pilgrimage" as the central thread, and a surrealist Franco-Indian love-story as his inspiration, he wrote his first novel, *Jaya Ganga, In Search of the River Goddess* (Ramsay 1985, Penguin 1989, Rupa 2005). The book received stupendous response from the entire French press.

Since then, Vijay Singh has written several books that have won wide critical acclaim internationally: *La Nuit Poignardée* (Flammarion, 1987), *Whirlpool of Shadows* (Jonathan Cape, 1992, Rupa 1992, 2005) and a dreamy tale for children, *The River Goddess* (Gallimard Jeunesse/Moonlight, 1994). *Whirlpool of Shadows* was listed by the 1992 Booker Prize Winner, Barry Unsworth, as one his three Best Books of the Year in *The Sunday Times*, UK.

Vijay Singh's entry into the world of images and cinema was pure accident. In 1989, a young French producer knocked at his door. He didn't have any specific project or film in mind, but he nevertheless insisted on doing a documentary with Vijay Singh. Singh's idea to make a documentary on the theme of man and animal led to the making of 'Man and Elephant', a 30′ film, part fiction part documentary, on the relationship between an elephant-keeper and his elephant in Kerala. To date, this film has been shown on over 100 televisions worldwide.

'Jaya Ganga' was Vijay Singh's first feature film, an adaptation of his earlier novel. It premiered in competition at the World Film Festival, Montreal, and then travelled to over 50 international festivals. It ran for 49 weeks in the Paris cinemas before playing on 80 screens in the UK. The film received tremendous press response internationally. *The Guardian* called it "a mesmerising film...One of the most authentic depictions of everyday Indian magic ever screened."

His second feature film, 'One Dollar Curry', was shot entirely in Paris and released in France and the UK. It ran to full houses for several weeks in North India and was highly acclaimed by the press.

Vijay Singh has been a guest speaker at several conferences held worldwide and has also made individual presentations of his work at the Universities of Harvard, Cambridge and Oxford. He has also held workshops for film students on "Literature and Cinema" at the Film and Television Institute of India, Pune.

He was awarded the Leonardo da Vinci Award for the screenplay of 'Jaya Ganga', La Titine Best Film Award for his documentary 'Man' and 'Elephant', and the Prix Villa Médicis hors les murs Award for foreign literature.

JHUMPA LAHIRI

Born in 1967

Jhumpa Lahiri is a famous Indian American author of Bengali origin. Her first novel, *The Namesake* was a major national bestseller and was named the New York Magazine Book of the Year. Jhumpa Lahiri became the first Asian to win the Pulitzer Prize when she won the 2000 Pulitzer Prize for fiction for her book *Interpreter of Maladies.*

Jhumpa Lahiri was born in July 1967 in London and was raised in Rhode Island. Jhumpa is an alumnus of Barnard College, where she received a B.A. in English literature, and of Boston University, where she received an M.A. in English, M.A. in Creative Writing and M.A. in Comparative Studies in Literature and the Arts, and a Ph.D. in Renaissance Studies. She took up a fellowship at Provincetown's Fine Arts Work Center for two years. Jhumpa Lahiri also taught creative writing at Boston University and Rhode Island School of Design.

Much of Jhumpa Lahiri's fiction deals with the lives of Indian-Americans, particularly Bengalis. Her debut collection *Interpreter of Maladies* won the 2000 Pulitzer Prize for fiction. It was a collection of nine distinct short stories addressing the sensitive dilemmas in the lives of Indians or Indian immigrants. *The Namesake,* her second book and first novel, came out in 2003. It was named the New York Magazine Book of the Year. Mira Nair is making an eponymous film based on the novel.

Lahiri, the daughter of a librarian and school teacher, has always been inclined to creative writing. Lahiri remembers a need to write as early as ten years old and she has always used writing as an outlet for her emotions, "When I learned to read, I felt the need to copy. I started writing ten page 'novels' during recess with my friends' writing allowed me to observe and make sense of things without having to participate. I didn't belong. I looked different and felt like an outsider" (Interview with Vibhuti Patel in *Newsweek International*, 9-20-99).

At a press conference in Kolkata in January of 2001, Lahiri described this absence of belonging, "No country is my motherland. I always find myself in exile in whichever country I travel to, that's why I was tempted to write something about those living their lives in exile". This idea of exile runs consistently throughout Lahiri's Pulitzer Prize winning book Interpreter of Maladies.

The book brings to light many of the issues with identity faced by the Diaspora community. The book contains the stories of first and second generation Indian immigrants, as well as a few stories involving ideas of otherness among communities in India. The stories revolve around the difficulties of relationships, communication and a loss of identity for those in diaspora. No matter where the story takes place, the characters struggle with the same feelings of exile and the struggle between the two worlds by which they are torn. The stories deal with the always shifting lines between gender, sexuality, and social status within a diaspora. Whether the character be a homeless woman from India or an Indian male student in the United States, all the characters display the effects of displacement in a diaspora.

Lahiri has won many awards for *Interpreter of Maladies*. These awards and honours include The Pulitzer Prize in 2000, The Transatlantic Review Award from the Henfield

Foundation, The Louisiana Review Award for Short Fiction, the O. Henry Award for Best American Short Stories, the PEN/Hemingway Award, The New Yorker Debut of the Year Award and The American Academy of Arts and Letters Award. Lahiri also received a nomination for the LA Times Book Prize as well as the Guggenheim Fellowship in 2002. She has published three stories in *The New Yorker*, as well as published works in the *Agni, Epoch, The Louisville Review, Harvard Review* and the *Story Quarterly*.

Lahiri is currently living in New York with her husband and son.

PANKAJ MISHRA

Born in 1969

Pankaj Mishra was born in North India in 1969. He graduated with a Bachelor of Commerce from the Allahabad University before completing his MA in English Literature at the Jawaharlal Nehru University in New Delhi. He wrote his first novel when he was only seventeen years old, and two further novels followed.

In 1992, he moved to Mashobra, a Himalayan village, where he began to contribute literary essays and reviews to *The Indian Review of Books, The India Magazine,* and the newspaper *The Pioneer*. His first book was *Butter Chicken in Ludhiana: Travels in Small Town India* (1995), a travelogue which described the social and cultural changes in India in the new context of globalization. His novel *The Romantics* (2000), an ironic tale of people longing for fulfilment in cultures other than their own, was published in eleven European languages and won the Los Angeles Times' Art Seidenbaum Award for first fiction. His recent book is *An End to Suffering.*

The Buddha in the World (2004), a New York Times notable book, mixes memoir, history, and philosophy while attempting to explore the Buddha's relevance to contemporary times. His most recent book, *Temptations of the West: How to be Modern in India, Pakistan and Beyond,* describes Mishra's travels through Kashmir, Bollywood, Afghanistan, Tibet, Nepal, and other parts of South and Central Asia. Like his previous books, it was featured in the New York Times' 100 Best Books of the Year.

In 2005, Mishra published an anthology of writing on India titled *India in Mind* (Vintage). His writings have been anthologized in *The Picador Book of Journeys* (2000), *The Vintage Book of Modern Indian Literature* (2004), and *Away: The Indian Writer as Expatriate* (Penguin), among other titles. He has introduced new editions of Rudyard Kipling's Kim (Modern Library), E. M. Forster's *A Passage to India* (Penguin Classics), J. G. Farrell's *The Siege of Krishnapur* (NYRB Classics), Gandhi's *The Story of My Experiments with Truth* (Penguin) and R. K. Narayan's *The Ramayana* (Penguin Classics). He has also introduced two volumes of V.S. Naipaul's essays, *The Writer and the World* and *Literary Occasions*.

Mishra writes literary and political essays for the *New York Times*, the *New York Review of Books, The Guardian*, and the *New Statesman*, among other American, British, and Indian publications. His work has also appeared in the *London Review of Books, Times Literary Supplement, Financial Times, Washington Post, Boston Globe, Time, The Independent, Granta, The Nation, N+1, Poetry, Common Knowledge, Outlook, Travel & Leisure, The New Yorker, and Harper's.* He was a visiting professor at Wellesley College in 2001, 2004, and 2006. In 2004-2005 he received a fellowship at the Cullmen Center for Writers and Scholars, New York Public Library. He divides his time between London and India and is presently on a Novel.

KIRAN DESAI

Born in 1971

Daughter of a well known Indian author, she is the winner of the 2006 Booker Prize. Well, we are talking about the eminent Indian novelist Kiran Desai. She was born on the 3rd of September in the year 1971 in Chandigarh. She spent the early years of her life in Pune and Mumbai. She studied in the Cathedral and John Connon School.

When she was around nine years old, her family shifted to Delhi. By the time, she turned fourteen, the family moved to England. A year later, they shifted to the United States. Kiran completed her schooling in Massachusetts. She did her graduation from Hollins University and Columbia University. Thereafter, she took a break of two years to write her first book *Hullabaloo in the Guava Orchard*.

This novel was published in the year 1998. It was an amazing piece of work, for which Kiran received many accolades. Her second book *The Inheritance of Loss* was also well acclaimed. She also received the 2006 Man Booker Prize and 2006 National Book Critics Circle Fiction Award for it.

With *The Inheritance of Loss*, Kiran Desai has become the youngest female laureate of the Booker Prize (2006). In her book she talks about exile, globalization and belonging to two cultures.

Criss-crossing the globe from Hay on Wye in Wales to Copenhagen, to Shanghai, Hong Kong, South Africa, Sri Lanka, Brazil, Canada, Indonesia, Desai laughingly describes her recent life as "living in cartoon form," where she hops from place to place.

Desai's new life is in stark contrast to the nearly eight years she spent toiling on the book that won her fame. "It was a long, long journey for me," she admits. "I was devastated and sad at the end of it." The often lonely process of writing was actually a happy one for her, she insists. Running out of money after she spent her publisher's advance and being too poor to afford health insurance or a place to call her own was not easy.

"I was quite stern and mean-spirited while writing the book, fearful of the risk I was taking," she explains. She hoped winning the Booker will change that, allowing her to be "more eccentric" and to "play more" when she writes again.

At first, Desai imagined that as time went by, she would feel more American than Indian, but she holds onto her Indian passport. "People are constantly asking me where home is, and after writing the book, I have less of an answer than ever before," she said.

"Literature is located beyond flags and anthems, simple ideas of loyalty," she feels. But working on the book led her back to India in many different ways. She felt "much more Indian" after writing the book than she had before. "Being part of the Indian diaspora gives one a precise emotional location to work from, if not a precise geographical one. This book was a return journey to the fact of being Indian, to realizing the perspective was too important to give up. America might give me half a narrative, but I had to return to India for the other half of the story, for emotional depth, historical depth."

"The book is movingly strong in its humanity... a magnificent novel of humane breadth and wisdom, comic tenderness and powerful political acuteness," observed the writer Hermione Lee, who headed the team of judges awarding the Booker to Desai, making her the youngest woman to win the award in its 40-year history.

Other Books on
GENERAL BOOKS

1.	Chanakya Neeti **(New)**	175/-
1.	Helpline for Stressed Parents **(New)**	175/-
2.	Grow Rich with Peace of Mind **(New)**	175/-
3.	How to be Fit and Young **(New)**	175/-
4.	How to Succeed in Life **(New)**	175/-
5.	100 Ways to Develop Self Confidence	160/-
6.	Child Development	195/-
7.	Abraham Lincoln A Complete Biography	195/-
8.	Mein Kampf My Struggle	195/-
9.	Think and Grow Rich	150/-
10.	The Art of Personality Development	150/-
11.	Positive Mind Power	160/-
12.	Travel & Tourism An Industry Facilitator	295/-
13.	World's Great Authors And Poets	150/-
14.	Effective Editing Help Yourself in Becoming a Good Editor	150/-
15.	Smart House-Keeping for Modern Women	150/-
16.	Develop Super Power Memory	125/-
17.	World's Great Personalities	160/-
18.	Personality Plus	150/-
19.	Power of Positive Thinking	150/-
20.	Art of Successful Parenting	175/-
21.	A Handbook of Etiquettes	125/-
22.	World's Great Scientists	150/-
23.	Body Language	125/-
24.	Art of Successful Living	150/-
25.	Jokes for All	125/-
26.	Selected Dohas	295/-
27.	Baby Names for Girls **(New)**	125/-
28.	Baby Names for Boys **(New)**	125/-
29.	Art of Public Speaking	150/-
30.	The World's Greatest Speeches	150/-
31.	Group Discussions	125/-
32.	Personality Development	110/-
33.	Think Positive & Things Will Go Right	110/-
34.	Once in a Blue Moon (A Tantra Tale)	125/-
35.	God is Dead	125/-
36.	Travel India (A Complete Guide for Tourists)	350/-
37.	Glimpses of Urdu Poetry	450/-
38.	How to Reduce Tension	125/-
39.	A Book of Stenography	295/-
40.	Baby Names for the Boy	125/-
41.	Baby Names for the Girl	125/-
42.	Ripples in Tranquil Waters	195/-

Unit No. 220, 2nd Floor, 4735/22, Prakash Deep Building,
Ansari Road, Darya Ganj, New Delhi- 110002
Ph.: 23280047, 9811594448
• E-mail : lotuspress1984@gmail.com, www.lotuspress.co.in